PRAISE FOR LORILYN ROBERTS

The author's writings will inspire her readers to be physically and spiritually prepared for the future.

— READERS' FAVORITE REVIEWER COURTNEE TURNER

I loved that the work carefully examines many aspects of life including daily, common events and life-altering global events. A voice for a new generation.

— READERS' FAVORITE REVIEWER EDITH WAIRIMU

These are powerful essays, written for times such as these. (As I write this review, Israel and Hamas are at war in Gaza. Chapter 42 of the book, "When They Cry, Peace and Safety," helps me make sense of the conflict.) Highly recommended.

— AUSTRALIAN NOVELIST MARTIN ROTH

GOD'S GOOD WORKS

Stories to Treasure and Tales to Ponder

LORILYN ROBERTS

God's Good Works: Stories to Treasure and Tales to Ponder

Copyright © 2023 Lorilyn Roberts

Rear Guard Publishing, Inc.

Gainesville, FL 32606

Ver 1.4

Cover photograph – standard licensing agreement

Cover design by Lisa Vento

Scripture taken from the NEW KING JAMES VERSION®. Copyright© 1982 by Thomas Nelson, Inc.

Library of Congress Control Number: 2023919943

ISBN: 979-8-9873394-3-5 (e-book)

ISBN: 979-8-9873394-4-2

ISBN: 979-8-9873394-5-9

Printed and bound in the United States of America

To My Dear Friend,

Becky Richburg

INTRODUCTION

"Now when He was asked by the Pharisees when the kingdom of God would come, He [Jesus] answered them and said, 'The kingdom of God does not come with observation; nor will they say, 'See here!' or 'See there!' For indeed, the kingdom of God is within you.'"
Luke 17:20-21

Dear Reader,

If you like inspiring devotionals that highlight the Kingdom of God and Jesus' imminent return, you will enjoy these "stories" I've shared over the last decade. The second half of the book focuses on the last three years and the Kingdom of Darkness. What does it mean considering Scripture and the soon return of our Lord and Savior?

Stories to Treasure include some of my most memorable moments and Godly insights over the years. They are vignettes, not quite devotionals and not quite memoirs. I seem to write books that are difficult to categorize. I enjoyed writing these spirit-filled stories until COVID-19 shut everything down in March 2020.

COVID-19 affected countries worldwide, not just here in the United States, and many well-meaning people seemed to have lost their sanity. I questioned everything. Perhaps I overthought what I perceived to be corrupt or even demonically-influenced decisions by our leaders. How do you make sense of the senseless? Especially when you feel you are in the minority. The second half of *God's Good Works - Tales to Ponder*, speaks to that perplexity.

Overnight, everything changed. As sports captioning disappeared from my calendar, local stores required masks, toilet paper was absent from store shelves, and I couldn't use cash, my writings became profoundly personal. I struggled to understand what was happening, and I found it challenging to find "Good" in any of it.

When I asked God what He wanted me to write after I finished my previous book, He said He wanted me to write about the darkness that began in 2020. I told God I didn't want to write about that. I didn't want to relive it. Besides, bookstores would censor a book like that—unless I was as wise as a serpent and harmless as a dove (Matthew 10:16).

The writer and philosopher George Santayana once said, "Those who cannot remember the past are condemned to repeat it."

I pray that none of us forget the last three and a half years, and the best way to ensure that doesn't happen is for people to record what they experienced.

If the survivors of World War II had remained silent, we wouldn't have a personal account of their stories and what truly happened behind those walls of secrecy. Do we want the government's version of "truth" to be our "legacy"? We must be bold and speak the truth so future generations won't say, "It didn't happen."

Despite my reticent spirit, what you hold in your hand is God's *Stories to Treasure and Tales to Ponder.* The darkness continues and is likely a foreshadowing of prophetic future events. If so, how would God call us to live if we have another catastrophic worldwide event? Ephesians 2:10:

> *"For we are His workmanship, created in Christ Jesus for good*
> *works, which God prepared beforehand that we should*
> *walk in them."*

Here's another quote from the New Testament that speaks to how we should live:

> *"When did we see You [Jesus] a stranger and take You in, or*
> *naked and clothe You? Or when did we see You sick, or in*
> *prison, and come to You?'*
> *"And the King will answer and say to them, 'Assuredly I say to*
> *you, inasmuch as you did it to one of the least of these My*
> *brethren, you did it to Me'" (Matthew 25:38-40).*

God has kept you and me here to occupy until He returns or until He calls us home. The Good News is Jesus is coming back. Just because it hasn't happened yet doesn't mean it won't. There is no reason to doubt God's promises.

> *"Nicodemus said to Him [Jesus], 'How can a man be born when*
> *he is old? Can he enter a second time into his mother's womb*
> *and be born?'*
> *"Jesus answered, 'Most assuredly, I say to you, unless one is born*
> *of water and the Spirit, he cannot enter the kingdom of*
> *God'" (John 3:4-5).*

Jesus and His disciples talked privately on the Mount of Olives in Matthew 24:3-4:

> *"Tell us, when will these things be? And what* will be *the sign of*
>   *Your coming, and of the end of the age?"*
> *"And Jesus answered and said to them:*
>   *'Take heed that no one deceives you.'"*

Jesus told His disciples in Matthew 24:24-25:

> *"For false christs and false prophets will rise and show great*
>   *signs and wonders to deceive, if possible, even the elect. See, I*
>   *have told you beforehand."*

Based on Jesus' words in this passage, I don't believe authentic Christians can be deceived. But if you don't know Jesus Christ, the devil's wiles can and most likely will. I urge you to make your calling sure. II Peter 1:10:

> *"Therefore, brethren, be even more diligent to make your call*
>   *and election sure, for if you do these things you will never*
>   *stumble;"*

We are God's ambassadors to share His Good News (II Corinthians 5:20). Our Good Works for the Kingdom of God will shine in the darkness as a witness, bringing hope where there is none.

The more we know God's truth, the darker this world will seem. And it will keep getting darker as the Powers of Darkness become more emboldened. Our spiritual battle is more extensive in scope than what we see. Those we see carrying out darkened schemes are either possessed by demons, demonically influenced, or demonically oppressed.

As Christians, we cannot win this battle in our flesh. Only through the Holy Spirit can we hold back the darkness. The Kingdom of God through the Holy Spirit is restraining the wickedness that will consume the world once God removes the true believers. Jesus said to Pontius Pilate:

> *"My kingdom is not of this world. If My kingdom were of this*

*world, My servants would fight, so that I should not be
delivered to the Jews; but now My kingdom is not from
here" (John 18:36).*

After Jesus died on the cross, fifty days later on Pentecost, God sent the Holy Spirit to indwell and fill the believers and help them shine the light of Jesus before men. That light is here today, and the darkness, no matter how dark it gets, can't extinguish God's eternal light (John 1:5). *Tales to Ponder* grapples with this Kingdom of Darkness.

How easy it is to forget where we've been over the last three and a half years. Who wants to remember it? There is a goal, however, to the madness we've witnessed. The globalists call it the New World Order.

Let me hasten to say the real New World Order is not of this world. The elitists use the title to draw attention to themselves and their human-projected creation of a fictional utopia. The real coming New World Order is the coming Kingdom of Heaven—God's Kingdom.

The Kingdom of Heaven will become a literal kingdom on Earth. King Yeshua (Jesus) will sit on His throne in Jerusalem and reign for a thousand years.

We often forget Jesus is a Jewish King, a Jewish Savior, and a Jewish God. The seven-year Tribulation is the time set on God's prophetic timetable to bring the Jews back to Israel so they can surrender to and embrace their Messiah—Yeshua Hamashiach.

Satan's Kingdom of Darkness will reach its zenith during the seven-year Tribulation.

> *"Alas! For that day is great, So that none is like it; And it is the
> time of Jacob's trouble, But he [Israel] shall be saved out of
> it" (Jeremiah 30:7).*

Because of the darkness, we can only catch glimpses of what's behind the veil. But like in *The Wizard of Oz*, when the little dog Toto pulls back the curtain, Jesus will pull back the veil when He returns. At last, He will execute justice, righteousness, and reign over the whole Earth (Zechariah 14:9).

In the darkness, *God's Good Works* are visible to those with eyes to see. The more you seek God, the more you find the Kingdom of God in others. The more you share *God's Good Works*, the more you bless others and store up treasures in the Kingdom of Heaven.

All things, hidden and unhidden, happen for a reason. Even human deception can have a purpose (Genesis 27).

In our humanity we often do not process traumatic events very well. Fear paralyzes us, and the enemy uses manipulative tactics to destroy our testimony.

> *"But he who fears has not been made perfect in love"*
> *(I John 4:18b).*
> *"...though I walk through the valley of the shadow of death, I*
>   *will fear no evil; For You [God] are with me"*
> *(Psalm: 23:4).*
> *"Therefore do not worry about tomorrow, for tomorrow will*
>   *worry about its own things. Sufficient for the day is its own*
>   *trouble"*
> *(Matthew 6:34).*

We are either Sons of God or sons of disobedience. The "prince of the power of the air" controls the Kingdom of Darkness and "...now works in the sons of disobedience..." (Ephesians 2:2).

As Sons of God, we are Children of Promise (Galatians 4:28). As Children of Promise, we're heirs in the future Millennial Kingdom (Galatians 4:7).

> *"For God is not unjust to forget your work and labor of love*
>   *which you have shown toward His name, in that you have*
>   *ministered to the saints, and do minister"*
> *(Hebrews 6:10).*

Will our country and world go back to the way it was before COVID-19? Or is this the new norm? Is this what the future holds for my children and yours?

When I'm saddened about the state of affairs, I remind myself I have much for which to be thankful. I need to put my hope in the One who died for you and me, our Lord and Savior. We are here for this time—to be God's witness in the Kingdom of Darkness. **To put our faith and trust in humans or politics is futile.**

My Heavenly Father also reminded me that those who are in power He put there. None of this craziness surprises Him. His purposes, thoughts, and plans are higher than ours.

> *"Fear not, for I* am *with you; Be not dismayed, for I* am *your God. I will strengthen you, Yes, I will help you, I will uphold you with My righteous right hand"*
> *(Isaiah 41:10).*

Our Christian testimony may be all of the Gospel some will ever see. We can be a light in the darkness, a beacon on a hill. We can speak a word of encouragement to those who are broken and pray for the hurting lost. We can get up in the morning and thank God for His faithfulness and sufficiency.

And today, at least, the sky isn't green. If I were a betting woman, I'm sure it won't be green tomorrow. God keeps order in the universe.

Some believe the "white horse" (Revelation 6:2) has been galloping across the Earth since March 2020. If true, the "red horse" (Revelation 6:4) is on the horizon.

Don't be dismayed when you read *Tales to Ponder* in the second half of *God's Good Works*. When Jesus returns, He will slay the Powers of Darkness with the breath of His mouth and the brightness of His coming (II Thessalonians 2:8).

We are not without hope because our hope extends beyond this world into the next. We know God wins, and the Kingdom of Heaven is near. Look up, our redemption is near. Satan's end is sure, and the most remarkable story ever written will have the most incredible ending imaginable!

PART ONE

Stories to Treasure

"God is not merely good, but Goodness; Goodness is not merely divine, but God."

~CS Lewis

Chapter One

DON'T BELIEVE THE LIES OF THE DEVIL

"He has delivered us from the power of darkness and conveyed us into the kingdom of the Son of His love."
Colossians 1:13

Many years ago, I watched a movie about a pastor who did not believe in the infallible Word of God. The passages he deemed irrelevant, he instructed his congregation to cut out of their Bibles. By the movie's end, the Bible was in rags, and when trials and tribulations came, those divinely inspired passages that the people needed were no longer in their Bibles.

If my pastor said during a Sunday morning sermon, "I think this Bible passage is wrong, and I will change it to..." I'd be looking for another church.

Anyone who tells me the Scriptures are flawed is not someone I would seek counsel from. We can only see through the glass darkly now, and while there are many things I don't fully understand, I know God will make it all clear on the last day.

While the movie is a fictional example of how the serpent can cause deception in a leader's understanding of Scripture, it's even more treacherous when the leader is the head of the Roman Catholic Church, including 1.2 billion Catholics.

For those unaware, Pope Francis in June 2019 officially approved changing the translation of the Lord's PRAYER found in Matthew 6:13 and Luke 11:4:

> *"And do **not lead us into temptation,** but deliver **us** from the evil one."*

To quote Pope Francis: "A father [doesn't lead his children into temptation]. A father helps you to get up immediately. It's Satan who leads us into temptation. That's his department."

The Pope's new rendition of the Lord's prayer to his Catholic followers is: "Do not let us fall into temptation."

This stunning proclamation by Pope Francis leads to other significant questions at the Gospel's core. Would a perfectly loving and Holy Father offer up His only begotten Son to be tortured, crucified, and killed as a sacrifice for humankind? Or what about when God commanded Abraham to offer up his only son, Isaac, as a sin offering?

What kind of example is Pope Francis setting when he says the Bible needs to be changed to comport with his understanding of what Jesus meant?

Examples abound in the Bible where Satan succeeded in his deception. Perhaps the most well-known is in Genesis 3:1:

> *"...And he [the serpent] said to the woman, 'Has God indeed said, 'You shall not eat of every tree of the garden?'"*

In another example, Satan misallocated Scripture when he tried to tempt Jesus three times in the wilderness. Jesus countered the serpent's false accusations by proclaiming, "It is written..."

Jesus says in Matthew 24:35:

> *"Heaven and earth will pass away, but My words will by no means pass away."*

By believing the Scriptures, even those parts that are difficult to understand, we can escape any temptation to reject or retranslate God's Word in a way we find palatable.

The Bible predicts that this is what will happen in the last days, that people will not be able to hear the Truth or accept it.

> *"For the time will come when they will not endure sound doctrine, but according to their own desires,* because *they have itching ears, they will heap up for themselves teachers; and they will turn* their *ears away from the truth, and be turned aside to fables"*
> *(Timothy 4:3).*

The Lord's prayer means what it says:

> *"And do **not lead us into temptation** but deliver **us** from the evil one."*

> *We can be sure whatever temptation we face, God will provide "the way of escape, that you may be able to bear* it" *(I Corinthians 10:13).*

None of us are equal to God or have the wisdom of God—including the Pope. Even if we try to remove or change something in God's Word, His Word will never pass away.

PRAYER: Our Father in Heaven, Hallowed be Your name. Your kingdom come. Your will be done on Earth as it is in Heaven. Give us this day our daily bread. And forgive us our debts, as we forgive our debtors. And do not lead us into temptation, but deliver us from the evil one. For Yours is the kingdom and the power and the glory forever. Amen.

Chapter Two

BLUEBIRDS AND SQUIRRELS AND THE GOODNESS OF THE LORD

"Look at the birds of the air, for they neither sow nor reap nor gather into barns; yet your heavenly Father feeds them. Are you not of more value than they? Which of you, by worrying can add one cubit to his stature?"
(Matthew 6:26-27)

For many summers, we had a nesting pair of birds that took up residence in the large Purple Martin house in our backyard. The Great Crested Flycatchers faithfully returned each year. We knew they had arrived when we heard them in the trees. If they thought I was watching, they would fly away.

Toward the end of summer, when the babies had fledged, the squirrels would move in and stay. When I took the Purple Martin house down at the end of the summer two summers ago, I found a large hole in the middle. The squirrels had remodeled the interior, and the flycatchers had enjoyed a mansion for a home.

I replaced it with a bluebird house the following spring. I wasn't sure if we would attract any bluebirds. When I saw a scout checking it out a few weeks later, I thought we might get lucky. After all, the birdhouse sits on prime real estate, like Park Place on the Monopoly board, with a bird's eye view of our pool; a canopy of honeysuckles, red tips, and water oak; and a small flower garden of shrimp plants, milkweed, and philodendrons. Much to my delight, the nesting pair parented multiple broods.

This year, I took a peek inside the house. I knew I should buy a new one. Only a plastic bag tie secured the warped base, but I was busy and forgot about it.

Soon bluebirds arrived and began building their nest. I watched them carry leaves, moss, and twigs into the hole. A few weeks later, I heard the faint sounds of babies. I was excited to watch the back-and-forth ritual of the parents feeding them. However, when a few days passed, and I didn't hear or see them, I became concerned. I looked around the front yard for any dead bluebirds.

I gave up the search when I saw the mother and father working on the nest again. They appeared to be undertaking a rebuilding project. Something must have gone awry, and they had started over.

Several days later, I went out for my daily swim. When I glanced at the wooden house, two beady eyes stared out of the dark hole. They were much too big to be a bluebird. Surprised, I examined it and noticed the enlarged opening. It was big enough for one determined squirrel to squeeze into, though it was a tight fit. The squirrel had usurped the bluebirds and now considered it her home.

I would have laughed if I hadn't seen the birds bringing in nesting material the day before. But what could I do? I got in the pool, distracted and concerned. Was the squirrel sitting on the eggs, or worse, smothering the babies?

After a while, I watched the male and female bluebirds fly to their nest. Suddenly, they halted their approach and flew over to a tree. They appeared to have no idea a squirrel was inside their quarters. I was upset because the squirrel had the entire canopy to build a nest.

I climbed out of the pool, grabbed the pole I used to skim the water, and angled it up to the birdhouse. The squirrel jumped out like he had been stung by a hornet. Wild eyes flashed as she scrambled past me, jumped from the fence into the thicket, and scurried off faster than a startled fish.

My job accomplished, I dipped back into the pool and swam to the far end. I hoped to see the bluebirds reclaim their territory, but they didn't return. Perhaps they were waiting for me to leave. It was getting dark anyway, so I got out, dried off, and went back inside to change.

Then I heard my daughter, Joy, scream, "Mamma, the bluebird house fell over."

"What?"

I ran out of the door. The box was partially burst open and lying on the ground. The squirrel must have broken the plastic tie scrambling out of the hole. Some nesting material had dislodged from the sides where the wooden boards had separated. I peered through the opening, searching for baby birds or eggs, but to my dismay, two baby squirrels were inside. I did a double-take because I expected to see birds. They were tiny with no hair and couldn't have been more than a few days old.

Would the mother return? How could the squirrel have been using the birdhouse? The baby squirrels didn't appear to be hurt. At least they were moving around a little, as much as babies with closed eyes can.

The nesting debris had cushioned the fall, though I wondered how so much "stuff" could fit into such a small space. We needed to figure out how to remount the birdhouse on the post. The base of it had rotted, and there was nothing to which we could mount it. I did manage to push the sides of the box back together.

I set the house on the table by the pool and went to the garage to find something we could use. Joy later told me she saw the mother squirrel return and leave. That was a good sign. I hoped that she would come back. I found a roll of sticky blue tape that we had used to cover the windows during the last hurricane season. We could use a screw to latch it on the post and run the tape around the sides and underneath it.

Joy and I climbed on top of the wooden fence and took turns pulling off tape and wrapping it like a Band-Aid. When we finished, it was nighttime, and we went back inside to watch.

A bluebird arrived immediately, but he refused to go in. He just sat outside the opening. We grew tired of watching the perched bird, and he was half-hidden in the trees anyway. I went to bed thinking about baby squirrels and feeling guilty for my part in the disaster. I wondered what I would do if the mother squirrel did not return.

The next day I kept an eye out for her, but the birdhouse just baked in the sun with no squirrel in sight. By late afternoon I had to do something. I took Joy to the gym and visited a friend who cared for orphaned animals.

I asked her if she would take the squirrels if I brought them to her. She reassured me she would. I ran home, climbed on the railing again, and brought the box down. I set it on the table and looked inside, but to my dismay, it was empty.

My friend said the mother might have returned that night or early in the morning. She explained that squirrels make several nests, so if ants overrun one nest or she is scared off, she has another one for nesting.

I still felt sorry for the bluebirds. I went to the store and bought a brand-new bluebird house that a determined squirrel couldn't gnaw through. My neighbor came over later that evening and anchored it so it couldn't get knocked over again. My biggest regret was that I didn't do it sooner.

Sometimes God paints pictures of life lessons that can have many meanings. I would have doubted my ability to raise a family if I were a bluebird. Would I even have the desire to try a third time?

If I were a squirrel, I would have learned it doesn't pay to steal someone else's home. I needed to build my own.

But God had a different message for me—things may not always be as they appear. While I was expecting bluebirds, God delivered squirrels.

How many times have I been so sure of myself only to find out later I was wrong? And maybe, just maybe, God wanted me to dive into the pool, enjoy a swim, and let Him take care of the bluebirds and the squirrels. God loves those little critters more than I do.

Despite my human limitations, I find joy in seeing the "Goodness of the Lord" in my backyard, all around me, and in the little things of life that are easy to disregard or ignore.

PRAYER; Please help us, Jesus, to see more of You in the Kingdom of God. Help us to rest, swim, and appreciate the fullness of Your Goodness here as we antici-pate what You have planned for us in Your Eternal Kingdom.

Chapter Three

THE DOOR TO GOD'S NEW WORLD ORDER

"And God will wipe away every tear from their eyes;"
Revelation 21:4

Today, I remind myself of the Heavenly home that awaits me. While my ability to change the world is limited, I can renew my thoughts and how I view the sometimes unexplained darkness. By allowing God to work in my heart through His Word, I can gain a Heavenly perspective, lifting me out of the gutter that often robs me of my joy.

Take a few moments and see what God is preparing. Our negative thoughts can be redeemed, helping us to live each day with renewed hope for a brighter future. Revelation 21:4:

"there shall be no more death, nor sorrow, nor crying. There shall
be no more pain, for the former things have passed away."

This New World Order will follow the greatest battle in the history of humankind. God and His angelic warriors will battle Satan and his fallen angels. Jerusalem will be the battleground, and our Redeemer's swift victory over Satan will usher in His rule as KING OF KINGS and LORD OF LORDS.

While we wait for Christ's return, God gives us glimpses of His Heavenly abode. It's a real, physical place outside of time inhabited by millions of angelic beings and living creatures. Our Savior, Jesus Christ, paid the extraordinary cost for our ticket. Only through His death on the cross can we enter. How great that cost—and Jesus did it for you and me.

Our King will reward His faithful servants. The most faithful ones will shine the brightest in Heaven, just like some stars are more brilliant in the night sky than others.

Heaven has no competition for food or toll for survival—even in the animal kingdom. Romans 8:22:

> *"For we know that the whole creation groans and labors with*
> *birth pangs together until now."*

> *"The wolf also shall dwell with the lamb,*
> *The leopard shall lie down with the young goat,*
> *The calf and the young lion and the fatling together*
> *And a little child shall lead them"*
> *(Isaiah 11:6.).*

> *"old things have passed away; behold, all things have*
> *become new"*
> *(II Corinthians 5:17).*

Darkness can't penetrate the Holy City because the glory of God gives it light (Revelation 21:11). After the New Jerusalem comes down from Heaven following the Battle of Armageddon, Jesus will reign and "tabernacle" with His family of believers in Jerusalem (Revelation 21:3).

Leviticus 26:12 prophesies:

> *"I will walk among you and be your God, and you shall be My*
> *people."*

The New Jerusalem, constructed of precious gold, will radiate with the majesty of God's splendor (Revelation 21:23). Precious gems will adorn the wall's foundations, and single pearls will make up each of the twelve gates (Revelation 21:21). Nothing impure will ever enter the city (Revelation 21:27).

A crystal clear river, the River of Life, will flow from God's throne (Revelation 22:1). The Tree of Life will be inside the city, bearing a different fruit each month. Its leaves will be for the healing of nations (Revelation 22:1-2).

As portrayed in Revelation, Heaven also has many mysteries. For example, the four winds that obey God and the four living creatures who unceasingly praise our Heavenly Father (Revelation 4:6).

The Bible does not reveal Heaven's exact location, but Genesis 28:12 gives a hint:

> *"Then he [Jacob] dreamed, and behold, a ladder was set up on*
> *the earth, and its top reached to Heaven; and there the*
> *angels of God were ascending and descending on it."*

In Revelation 4:1, John sees an open door to Heaven. Acts 7:56, Stephen says:

> *"Look! I see the Heavens opened and the Son of Man standing at*
> *the right hand of God!"*

Because nothing defiled or sinful can enter Heaven, it would have been impossible for anyone to go there if God had not provided a way.

Long ago, God cast Satan and his minions out of Heaven, and today, we battle against these powers of darkness. But through the Holy Spirit, we can taste Heaven here. The Spirit whispers to us in our sleep, comforts us in our pain, and implores us never to give up. The Bible reminds us of the unwavering truth that even the rocks would cry out in praise to our Heavenly Father if it were possible (Luke 19:40).

When Jesus hung on the cross, He said to one of the two thieves beside Him:

"Assuredly, I say to you, today you will be with Me in Paradise"
(Luke 23:43).

Jesus has been preparing a place for those who believe in Him for the last two thousand years (John 14:3).

"For now we see only a reflection as in a mirror; then we shall
see face to face. Now I know in part; then I shall know fully,
even as I also am fully known"
(I Corinthians 13:12).

My translation of this passage in today's "jargon," now we see through a glass darkly, but someday Heaven will be fully known to us, even as we are fully known to God.

I look forward to hearing the Heavens declare the glory of God (Psalm 19:1), drinking from the living fountains of waters (Revelation 7:17), and walking with Jesus in the New Jerusalem (Revelation 21:3).

I recently traveled to Israel, and toward the end of the trip, I felt this longing I couldn't explain. As I thought about it, I realized what I wanted was Jesus. While visiting the Holy Land is an incredible experience, Jesus isn't physically present. His presence is through the Holy Spirit. I contemplated seeing Jesus seated on His throne, reigning from Jerusalem, as He will do when He establishes His millennial Kingdom.

I look forward to meeting believers who have gone before us and feasting at the marriage supper of the Lamb. Everyone's name, written in the Book of Life, will see the face of God (Revelation 22:4).

A glorious eternity awaits us. Let not the heartaches of this world discourage us from remembering the richness of God's grace even now —found in Jesus Christ. God sent His only Son to die on the cross for us so we might have eternal life. As Jesus said in John 16:33:

"In the world, you will have tribulation; but be of good cheer, I
have overcome the world."

PRAYER: Please, help us, Heavenly Father, to keep our eyes focused on You.
Despite trials, hardships, difficulties, and distractions, may we remember these

afflictions are temporary, and a Heavenly home awaits us where there will be no more tears, crying, or sorrow.

Chapter Four

BUILDING A KINGDOM AT THE TOP OF THE WORLD

"Of the increase of His government and peace there will be
    no end,
Upon the throne of David and over His kingdom,
To order it and establish it with judgment and justice
From that time forward, even forever.
The zeal of the LORD will perform this."
Isaiah 9:7

After spending a week in Nepal, I appreciate the little things so much more. I can drink tap water, enjoy coffee with breakfast, and eat anything I want. The air is clean, and I can sleep in my own bed. I know this sounds trite, and I don't mean it to be. God uses the mundane things in this world to teach us about the extraordinary world in the next.

We live in worlds of comfort zones. Home is our familiar world, but it's temporary. My little abode is in sunny Florida, where we have far too many cats that we fostered and couldn't part with and a rescued dog. Most of my friends live nearby, and it's where I work and play and do too much complaining about meaningless things.

Most of Nepali culture was unfamiliar to me. What made it

familiar were the relationships with the Christians I met. While there, we praised the same God, sang the same songs, and enjoyed the sweet fellowship of Nepali Christians in their homes and places of worship.

Where will your future home be?

Jesus said, "I go and prepare a place for you."

In Matthew 16:19, He also said:

> *"I will give you the keys of the kingdom of heaven, and what-*
> *ever you bind on earth will be bound in heaven, and what-*
> *ever you loose on earth will be loosed in heaven."*

God numbers our days, and we can't take anything with us when we leave this world. What will matter will be what we did for God. Investing time, money, talent, and knowledge into His Kingdom here will pay dividends in the Kingdom of Heaven.

Of course, if you aren't a Christian, you will never enter the Kingdom of Heaven. You've chosen not to be part of that world, intentionally or unintentionally. If you don't want to praise and worship the Savior here, you wouldn't want to do so there. Heaven would be outside of your comfort zone. That familiarity begins here on Earth in our spiritual relationships rooted in Jesus Christ. Those relationships are eternal, and the binding of those relationships here will also be bound in Heaven.

Why have you rejected the most crucial relationship this side of eternity? Jesus Christ died on the cross so you could live with Him forever.

Nothing familiar will exist in hell, either. Hell was made for the devil and his fallen angels—not for humans. Although, perhaps, one thing might be a tad familiar—loneliness. What would it be like always to be alone? I would imagine in hell, you're alone because God made us to be in relationships with Him and other people. Hell is everything Heaven isn't.

God created humans because He wanted a family on Earth, as He had one in Heaven. In the Kingdom of God, our forged relationships will continue into eternity, and whatever those relationships are here will be much more so there.

Despite how hard things can be sometimes, let us not grow weary of doing good. Let's demonstrate that we are God's extraordinary workmanship (Galatians 6:9). While worldly pursuits provide for Earthly needs, our works for the Kingdom of God are the building blocks for the Kingdom of Heaven. That Kingdom is without end. It won't burn up, collect dust, rot, or become outdated. Our Good Works are reaping an eternal award far more valuable than gold or silver (I Peter 1:7).

Before I went to Nepal, I allowed the evil one to convince me otherwise. Now, I see the Kingdom of God here with more hope and belief in the impossible.

> *"For since the beginning of the world*
> Men *have not heard nor perceived by the ear,*
> *Nor has the eye seen any God besides You,*
> *Who acts for the one who waits for Him"*
> *(Isaiah 64:4).*

God's Kingdom is expanding, and the Blessed Hope is nearer today than yesterday. Nothing except our unbelief can prevent God's power from manifesting in our hearts. Seize the moment and make your Earthly home a "taste" of your Heavenly home. What more excellent gift can we give our family than a preview of what's to come?

Despite the uptick in evil these last days, inwardly, God is renewing us for His glory.

If you aren't a Christian, why aren't you? The Kingdom of God calls our name and woos us as a lover woos his beloved. Can you hear Him whispering in your ear? God loves you. You're only a heartbeat away from eternity. Today is the day of salvation.

PRAYER: Please help us, Jesus, to remember You in the mundane, the extraordinary, the unpredictable, and the unknown. Help us to stay so close to You if You call our name, we will hear Your voice. And may it be a precious sound in our ears.

Chapter Five

BORN AGAIN IN THE KINGDOM OF GOD

"Jesus answered and said to him [Nicodemus], 'Most assuredly, I
say to you, unless one is born again, he cannot see the
kingdom of God.'"
John 3:3

What would it have been like to live in the Garden of Eden? I used to think it was gone forever because I didn't understand what God had planned for us in the future. I didn't know His-Story.

But all is not lost. A thread of love, perhaps hidden in our DNA, joins the perfect world that was (the Garden of Eden), the tainted world that is (the Kingdom of Darkness), and the redeemed world of the future (the Kingdom of Heaven). The Bible has a three-act structure, just like all good books.

All good books have a theme woven through the pages. The author will deliver the "goods" in the final chapter if the book is well-written. In the same way, God has woven His-Story from creation to fall to redemption to restoration.

No good author would pen a book without knowing how the story ends. God's Book of sixty-six chapters was written by prophets and scribes who painstakingly penned the words thousands of years ago.

The Bible has the most remarkable ending of any book ever written. And, in case you didn't know, God is also a best-selling author. The Bible has sold more books than any other book in the history of humankind.

> "...looking unto Jesus, the author and finisher of our faith;
> who for the joy that was set before Him endured the cross,
> despising the shame, and has sat down at the right hand of
> the throne of God"
> (Hebrews 12:2).

God used many writing tools to create His-Story. Some chapters He wrote as poetry.

> "But now ask the beasts, and they will teach you;
> And the birds of the air, and they will tell you;
> Or speak to the earth, and it will teach you;
> And the fish of the sea will explain to you;
> Who among all these does not know
> That the hand of the LORD has done this,
> In whose hand is the life of every living thing,
> And the breath of all mankind"
> (Job 12:7)?

As a Christian author, when I look for Goodness, I feel His-Story in verse:

> Long ago,
> in the Garden of Eden,
> I imagine sunsets dancing to colors our eyes cannot see
> and waterfalls trumpeting God's ownership over the Earth.
> Rocks proclaiming His glory
> and flowers singing His praises.
> The Earth's crust beneath our feet
> hints at His creations from ages past.
> The stars that shine as angels in the night sky

proclaim His lordship over every living creature.
The winds that mount on eagles' wings
fill the Earth with
His Spirit of redemption. [1]

Poetry seeps into our souls and speaks to our hearts where the Holy Spirit dwells.

Good books also have a page-turning event at about the midway point. Everything has been building to that scene, and when the event takes place, the pieces fall into place.

However, the ending is not yet sure. Will it turn out the way the protagonist wants?

In God's Book, Jesus' death and resurrection is His-Story's turning point. And when He sent the Holy Spirit at Pentecost, His-Story set up the final act.

For authors, at this point, the protagonist's transformation will give him the tools or the ability to reach the book's stated end goal—if he perseveres.

The Bible follows the Three-Act Paradigm just like any good book should. In the New Testament, Jesus' death on the cross and resurrection set the stage for Act Three (Tribulation). The pieces fit naturally into place: More prophetic signs are uncovered and fulfilled as we reach the end.

Authors refer to these as clues, hints, and techniques to keep the reader engaged and reading until the very last page.

After we're born again, like a small child, we must grow in the Lord. The process is called sanctification. For the church, the world is the mission field. Christians call it The Great Commission—to go out and make disciples.

> *"And Jesus came and spoke to them, saying, 'All authority has been given to Me in heaven and on earth. Go therefore and make disciples of all the nations, baptizing them in the name of the Father and of the Son and the Holy Spirit, teaching them to observe all things that I have commanded you; and lo, I am with you always, even to the end of the age'"*

(Matthew 28:18-20).

It would be a boring book if nothing happened in Act Three, what authors call the Denouement.

I am comforted that in Act Two of my life, God hasn't wasted anything. The little subplots, twists, and turns come together into a glorious ending. I've made it my life's goal to find redemption in all the valleys. Otherwise, I may not reach the next mountaintop. We must walk through the valley before we can climb the next mountain. If I can do that (including forgiving others, a part of sanctification), then God can use my redemptive failures.

As Jesus said, we will see the Kingdom of God when we are born again. If you want the best seat in the house, in the theater, or wherever you are reading, watching, praying, and communing, punch your ticket now. Be born again by giving your life to Jesus.

Clean up your life and begin the first day of the rest of your life. And when the final chapter unfolds, you will see the face of God. Be with Him to celebrate, and see your name in the credits of the Greatest Story ever told when God unseals the scroll.

PRAYER: Please help us, Jesus, to take every thought captive and help us to use every opportunity You give us for Your glory. As born-again newbies, please help us to be Your ambassadors for Good in this fallen world.

Chapter Six

SCUBA DIVING OFF THE TURNIFFE ISLANDS

*"Finally, my brethren, be strong in the Lord and in the power of
    His might.
Put on the whole armor of God, that you may be able to stand
    against the wiles of the devil."*
Ephesians 6:10-11

Scuba diving is not for the faint of heart. But my desire to see God's
beauty underneath the ocean outweighed my apprehension of what
could happen. While it's been many years since I have scuba-dived, one
dive is very memorable.

I was on a trip with my diving friends off the Turniffe Islands near
Belize. Whatever I had for lunch that day didn't agree with me, but I
wasn't willing to miss the dive. I packed my diving gear—tank, octopus,
BC, mask, fins, and snorkel— made sure I had 3,500 pounds of
compressed air in the tank, and released some of the air from the regulator to ensure it was working correctly. I was good to go in every way
except one.

My buddy and I jumped off the back of the dive boat and began our
descent, equalizing the pressure in our ears on the way down. We
descended to fifty feet, and I gave the thumbs-up signal for "I am

okay." The high-definition Blu-ray cinematography was exhilarating. Multi-colored coral, sea anemones, blue damsels, grouper, and the occasional eel and nurse shark were familiar sights on the dives. I often wondered why God would create a world under the ocean with so much perfection that most would never see.

However, as much as I wanted to enjoy the dive, my stomach was flip-flopping. I swam over to hide behind some red fire coral. Like a lit firecracker, my lunch burst through my regulator in a spectacular display, falling like ash all around me. I expected the regurgitated food to disappear into the ocean's abyss, but I was fifty feet down and weightless with my BC. Clumps of half-digested food floated in my face.

I looked past the mess to see my dive buddy approaching. I motioned him away, but he didn't know what I meant. As he neared, particles floated between our face masks. If only he knew what was floating around us, but I didn't tell him.

Reflecting on that unpleasant experience, I see sin being like that. We live with evil our entire lives. It surrounds us, torments us, and we can become so close to it we don't even recognize it.

Sin not only entangles us, but it will destroy us without the tools God gives us, as described in Ephesians 6.

On many dives, I never felt closer to God than in the quietness of the ocean's depths. But on that particular day, amid all God's beauty, undigested food floated within inches of my face, and I didn't feel close to God.

Sin lurks in this world everywhere. Perhaps guardian angels protect us more than we realize. But the tools God has given us will defeat evil, the devil, and his minions every time we employ them.

Do we not sometimes drift along in our spiritual life, like on a dive, unaware of our perilous condition because we have gotten lazy, complacent, or have given into some sin?

Jesus bore our sins on the cross so we could receive forgiveness and spend eternity with Him. I have contemplated on occasion, if I were the only human God created, He would have sent His Son to die for me. In my limited Earthly understanding, knowing my sinful, rebellious heart, I can't fathom that kind of grace. I am too small, and He is too big.

Without Jesus Christ, we are all eternally doomed. It is easy to say we are Christians, love the Lord and want to live for Him. If we are halfway decent Christians, we will read our Bible and pray daily, bless our food at mealtimes, attend church regularly, and be kind to our family and others, thanking God for His blessings.

But if that is all we do, would it entitle us to be included in chapter eleven of Hebrews' list of heroes? Are we willing to sacrifice our lives for Him?

Foxe's Book of Martyrs gives striking examples of Christians who paid the ultimate price, but radical Christianity can also express itself without dying. What is our testimony? Can we say God has transformed our lives into something remarkable for the Kingdom? Can we share the sacrifices we've made to encourage others? Are we imitators of Goodness that brings glory to God?

When Jesus was in the wilderness for forty days and forty nights, He was weakened physically by fasting. It was then Satan tempted Him. Satan knows when we're weak.

In times of temptation, if we pray and do what God has told us in Ephesians 6, He will pour out His protection, filling our hearts with His love and enabling us to escape the devil's wiles.

After that dive, I returned to the boat and rested. God took care of me on that day, a reminder that in this sinful world, God will come alongside us and give us rest after a spiritual battle.

If we look for Goodness, God can redeem our failures and our flaws. He can use even the lowly things for His glory.

PRAYER: Please help us, Lord, to call on You when sin threatens to hurt us or those whom we love. Even in the darkness, please help us to see Your Goodness. Help us to love You more and this world less.

Chapter Seven

WRETCHED, PITIFUL, POOR, BLIND, AND NAKED

"So then, because you are lukewarm, and neither cold nor hot, I
   will vomit you out of My mouth."
Revelation 3:16

Recently I watched several YouTube videos about injured or abandoned dogs and cats. Most of the stories were heartbreaking. And yet, frequently, with intervention, the unfortunate four-legged creature underwent a spectacular transformation. Sadly, I imagine for every video I've watched where the outcome is miraculous, hundreds die in misery because they never receive the care they need.

Sometimes when I see an animal video come up on my YouTube feed, the animal looks beyond hope, beyond healing, beyond the effort it would take to save him. At times, I ask myself, why do I watch these videos? The sorrow will break my heart, and I don't want to feel their pain. Ignoring those gut-wrenching videos and searching for something less emotional would be much easier. Sometimes I do that. "I can't handle it tonight," I say to myself. "I'm worn out fighting my own battles. Watching that video will drain me and make me depressed."

However, when a rescuer saves an animal, I am reminded of Goodness. We forget the financial, emotional, and spiritual costs oftentimes require a huge commitment on the part of the rescuer. Once, I watched a rescued dog die unexpectedly. I was distraught, and so were the people involved in the rescue. I felt the intense pain of losing the dog and the rescuers' sorrow because they grieved over an animal they had labored to save.

I often post these videos on Twitter, so if I want to watch them later, I can easily find them. Recently, I posted a video of a dog on Facebook that was the most emaciated dog I had ever seen. I couldn't imagine the dog would survive, but he did, and the rescue organization found a home for him. The video had one of those happily-ever-after endings that we all want for ourselves and those we love.

After posting the video on Facebook, I went to my page a few days later to read the comments; there were none. So I posted a follow-up comment: "Only one person liked this video, and it's such an amazing transformation. Be blessed."

It's been two weeks, and no one has given the video a thumbs-up. I am saddened. A good Samaritan saves a dog's life, and even with coaxing, I can't get anyone to watch it. In the past, I've posted about snake encounters, and I would get up to a hundred comments or likes. Is this the world we live in? No one gives a second thought about a rescued dog, but share a meaningless snake video, and everyone has something to say?

I've watched the video of the dog many times. When I see him, I see myself. "I once was lost, but now am found, was blind, but now I see."[1]

Jesus warned us in the Book of Revelation that the church in the days before His return would be neither cold nor hot. He describes the church as lukewarm—preoccupied with the things of this world, lacking empathy, and gloating over material wealth. While the Laodicean church believed they needed nothing,

God saw them as:

"..wretched, miserable, poor, blind, and naked—" (Revelation 3:17).

What an indictment! We aren't even talking about unbelievers. We're talking about Christians.

I'm reminded "white garments" symbolize holiness. God's holiness sees what we can become, not what we are now. According to Revelation 3:5, many in Heaven will wear holy white garments:

> *"He who overcomes shall be clothed in white garments, and I will not blot out his name from the Book of Life; but I will confess his name before My Father and before His angels."*

A Good Samaritan rescued that pitiful dog because he knew what the dog could become if he gave the poor creature food, medicine, and love. The starving dog in the YouTube video had no hope—until someone gave him reason to hope. And God has done the same for us.

God admonishes us to be like Him. When He saved us, we were wretched, but our Lord didn't see that. He saw what He created us to be. God saw the future you and the end me—a time when we would be awakened from our slumber and made alive through the Holy Spirit.

Can we be like Jesus and show compassion for someone or something in need? Can we be like the person who rescued that dog or others who have rescued animals or people? Am I willing to take time out of my busy schedule to do something for the Kingdom?

As Jesus said in Matthew 9:37:

> *"The harvest truly is plentiful, but the workers are few."*

Psalm 22:6 is a prophetic statement attributed to Jesus:

> *"But I am a worm, and no man; a reproach of men, and despised by the people."*

It is easy to disregard something disturbing. Only by the healing salve of Jesus can our eyes be opened. Only then will we appreciate the depth and breadth of God's love and His sacrificial death on the cross. And if we are still human, hopefully, we can empathize with those who are hurting and need help.

In the busyness of living, will we seek a comfortable Christianity and live in blissful ignorance, ignoring the pain of others?

God can use us when we're willing to be set aside, inconvenienced, and humbled. When we embrace suffering, we come to the end of ourselves. God reminds us of His sufficiency and our dependency on Him.

Can we take time to pray? Can we take time to listen? Can we take time to watch a video that might seem insignificant? If we do, God will redeem that time and renew us in His image for His glory.

PRAYER: Dear Jesus, please help us to remember in everything we do to give You all the honor and all the glory.

Chapter Eight

THE NEXT MAN UP, ARE YOU READY?

"Preach the word! Be ready in season and out of season.
Convince, rebuke, exhort, with all long-suffering and
teaching."
(II Timothy 4:2)

I've often thought about the parallels we can draw between sports and the Christian faith. To give an excellent example, a few years ago, I captioned a college football game, Kennesaw State University versus Wofford.

One thing that made captioning this game unique is I attended Kennesaw State University eons ago when I took an American history class. I've always been a history buff, even when I didn't know I was one.

For those unfamiliar with Kennesaw State University, it's located in Kennesaw, Georgia, about twenty miles north of Atlanta. The school has an enrollment of approximately 30,000 students, and the football team, known as the Owls, is a recent entry into the Big South Conference.

On this day, the Owls and the Wofford Terriers squared off in the first round of the FCS playoffs. I've captioned hundreds of games in every sport imaginable over the past twenty years, but midway through the second quarter, the ordinary game became extraordinary—at least for me.

Kennesaw State's star quarterback Tommy Bryant suffered an injury and had to leave the game. Tommy had played every second of every football game for the entire season. Jonathan Murphy, the backup quarterback, had not taken a single snap. For twelve weeks, he sat on the sidelines and watched.

I'd seen this scenario dozens of times before. A team works their tails off to make it to the playoffs only to have their star player go down, and their dreams of winning a championship go down with him.

So, I didn't expect this game to be any different. In the first possession, the team often panics, fumbles the ball, and the opponent picks it up and runs down the field for a touchdown.

But not this time. This unknown backup quarterback took over like he had been playing all season, leading Kennesaw State to a 28-21 playoff victory. In the process, Jonathan set several records, including running for 206 yards, the most by a quarterback in conference playoff history.

As I captioned the game, I began to think about that young man, Jonathan Murphy. The Owls played their first game against Point University on August 31. From August 31 to November 30, Jonathan watched from the sidelines. Every week for three months, he practiced with his team, knowing that his chances of even entering the game were slim, but he had to be ready if called upon at a moment's notice. If Tommy Bryant became sick or injured, Jonathan Murphy was the next man up.

Week after week, he practiced.

I never participated in sports at that level when I was young, but my daughter competed for years in gymnastics. From a distance, I could imagine Jonathan's time commitment to conditioning and practicing. I know the sacrifice it takes, the perseverance, and the determination to be the best.

I don't know if I could be that self-sacrificing for my team. I'd want to be in the game. Maybe I might work hard for the first month, but toward the end of the season, I'd be depressed. Perhaps I'd lose interest. But not Jonathan Murphy. He was ready.

Inspiration and insight came to me when the game was over. Is the Christian life not like that? We go for periods without trials and tribulations. Life is good. And then something happens, and life is not good. Life is hard. Are we ready when those times come?

It's not enough to just be ready when God calls us to step up—we need to be spectacularly ready, like Jonathan Murphy when he came on the field and led his team to victory.

Can we sit on the sidelines and be tempted to think God doesn't need us? Perhaps we slack off on our daily Bible reading or quit talking to God. Maybe we become a little worldly in our thoughts, or we lose that fire in our belly for the things of God. Are we willing to diligently work hard for Christ even if we don't get noticed?

Sometimes, when working on a book, I wonder if anyone will ever read it. I remind myself when the evil one gets in my ear, "I write for an audience of one."

In my twenty years of captioning, I don't believe I have ever seen a young man come into a game like that, who had not played all season and play so brilliantly. If anything, his poise and readiness inspired me to look into my own heart and tell God, "I want to be that person for You, to be ready at a moment's notice if called upon, always proclaiming Your Word in season and out of season, living my life for You, even when life is dull.

Let's face it. Most of life is pretty mundane, but we never know when God will call us from the sidelines to be His man or woman of the hour. You or I might be God's next man up.

PRAYER: I pray that we'll be ready.

Chapter Nine

BE STILL AND KNOW THAT I AM GOD

"Be still, and know that I am God."
Psalm 46:10

As I was prepped for my third round of proton therapy for breast cancer, I reached up to grab the overhead bars. Once the technician positioned me, he said, "Don't move." As he closed the treatment room door, I waited for the cancer-killing machine to sound.

The equipment started and stopped over and over. My arms became spastic and tired. When the machine finally finished, I broke into tears. I hadn't moved for two hours. Later, my daughter dropped off some cards from friends to encourage me.

A Bible verse was among the cards:

"He [God] says, "Be still, and know that I am God."

While I never had to stay immobile for that long again, the discipline of being still showed me how difficult it can be in times of stress and uncertainty.

I could have heard a pin drop in that room, all alone and motionless. God didn't need to shout to get my attention. As I struggled to get through that challenging round of proton therapy, I heard His comforting, gentle voice.

Now that my life is back to "normal" following cancer and COVID-19, I see once again how the tyranny of the urgent can consume me. I must remember to take quiet moments to recharge, refocus, and not become stressed. And when those challenging days come, as they always will, I will hear God's voice and take comfort in knowing I'm not alone.

PRAYER: Our Father, please help us to be still when we need to be still. Help us to hear Your voice even when things seem overwhelming. Knowing You are by our side brings comfort when we need it most.

Chapter Ten

KNOWLEDGE SHALL INCREASE

"But you, Daniel, shut up the words, and seal the book until the time of the end; many shall run to and fro, and knowledge shall increase."
Daniel 12:4

The information available at our fingertips has exploded in the last few years. Scientists tell us until the early 1900s, knowledge doubled every hundred years. That rate increased by the end of 1945 to once every twenty-five years. In today's world, thanks to the Internet, it happens every twelve hours!

Examples of the exponential increase in technology are endless. The Chinese robot, Sophia, is the most advanced robot ever created. We ask Seri and Alexa questions as if they are human and smarter than we are.

With the introduction of ChatGPT, we now have A.I. that can write chapters, sermons, songs, and poetry. When asked to write a full-length sci-fi book, it crashed, claiming the "lack of resources," but given enough time, I imagine it will write many books. What else will A.I. be able to do?

Even before ChatGPT, technological advancements boggled the

mind. Because of technology, we don't need wires running through the house to connect us to the other side of the world. We can call anywhere for free, send an email, or enjoy videos and jpegs on social networking sites from Antarctica to Timbuktu.

Today, most of the information sharing occurs on the Worldwide Web. Scientists predict this super-information highway will eventually connect everyone to each other on the globe.

The three "W's" in Worldwide Web represent the letter Vav, the sixth letter in the Hebrew alphabet. Is there any coincidence that www., the symbol for the Worldwide Web, becomes 666 when switched to a numerical value in Hebrew?

Interesting questions arise because today's number one source for information occurs on a platform symbolized in Hebrew by 666. To quote Sir Francis Bacon, "Information is power," but to also quote a well-respected British politician, Lord Action, "Absolute power corrupts absolutely."

Many Christians know the number 666 is associated with the most powerful ruler (Antichrist) who will walk the Earth. He will control the information highway, including all buying and selling. Those who want to survive will be forced to receive his mark on their right hand or forehead (Revelation 13:16).

Satan's deception will come through this lawless one, and millions of Earth-dwellers will do his bidding due to lack of knowledge. Hosea 4:6 states, "My people are destroyed for lack of knowledge." The minds of unbelievers will be blinded, and because of hardened hearts, God will send a strong delusion that, if it were possible, would deceive even the elect (II Thessalonians 2:11).

Too many will believe the lie (II Thessalonians 2:10). Some will be lured away from God because of their own desires (James 1:14). Others will not be willing to endure sound teaching (II Timothy 4:3). We live in a "me-my-mine" world, where people believe they are entitled to what someone else has (Galatians 5:20), are easily offended (Matthew 24:10), and are self-indulgent (II Timothy 3:2). Truth is relative and moral values are inverted (II Peter 2:2). Evil is called good, and good is called evil (Isaiah 5:20).

When the Bible refers to "knowledge" in Daniel 12:4, the context refers not only to man's knowledge bolstered by artificial intelligence but also to spiritual discernment.

God's promises include discernment that will help us to know the difference, for example, between real and fake news, what's right and wrong, absolute truth and relative truth, and good and evil (Hosea 14:9).

This wisdom will be significant and compelling, and only those who are enlightened with the knowledge of Jesus Christ will understand what is happening as the Day of the Lord approaches.

> *"My son, if you receive my words,*
> *And treasure my commands within you,*
> *So that you incline your ear to wisdom,*
> And *apply your heart to understanding:*
> *Yes, if you cry out for discernment,*
> And *lift up your voice for understanding,*
> *If you seek her as silver,*
> *And search for her as* for *hidden treasures;*
> *Then you will understand the fear of the LORD,*
> *And find knowledge of God.*
> *For the LORD gives wisdom;*
> *From His mouth* come *knowledge and understanding;"*
> *(Proverbs 2:1-6)*

The Apostle Paul says in Romans 12:2:

> *"And do not be conformed to this world, but be transformed by the renewing of your mind, that you may prove what* is *that good and acceptable and perfect will of God."*

Many don't know that God created both good and evil (Isaiah 45:7). He put the Tree of the Knowledge of Good and Evil in the Garden of Eden (Genesis 2:9). Just as God tested Adam and Eve, a time of shaking is coming upon the Earth to separate the wheat from the tares —those who love the truth from those who love the darkness (Matthew 13:30).

Where evil abounds, God abounds more (Romans 5:20). All manner of God's wisdom in understanding, art, and craftsmanship will be magnified (I Peter 4:11). God only requires our upmost obedience (Jeremiah 7:23). By faithfully following our Lord and Savior, seasoned with love, we will understand all knowledge and all mysteries (I Corinthians 13:1).

No matter how dire the circumstances, the Word of the Lord is forever (Isaiah 40:8). God's wisdom is sweet, like manna from Heaven (Proverbs 24:14). Knowledge of the Lord will be as the waters cover the sea (Isaiah 11:9), and God will reveal the mysteries sealed long ago (Revelation 6:1). We can take heart that those who love Jesus will be full of the knowledge of the glory of the Lord from now into eternity (Habakkuk 2:14).

PRAYER: Please help us, Jesus, to remain faithful if You tarry. Help us to finish well so we can receive Your affirmation, "Well done, my good and faithful servant."

Chapter Eleven

WHAT NO EYE HAS SEEN

"But as it is written:
'Eye has not seen, nor ear heard,
nor have entered into the heart of man
The things which God has prepared for those who love Him.'"
I Corinthians 2:9

Many years ago, I traveled to Nepal to adopt my first child. Nepal, located between India and China, is one of the poorest countries in the world. I had waited many years to become a mother, and now, as a single woman, I felt God leading me to adopt a three-year-old girl. Her mother had died, and her father could not provide for her.

I arrived in Kathmandu, trusting God to lead the way. I was sure He would go before me, and I had no reason to doubt I would go home with my new daughter. But after two weeks of bureaucratic delays and attempted bribery, the official in a small community near the border of China, high in the Himalayan Mountains, denied the adoption.

My hope that God would give me a daughter seemed impossible despite my prayers and friends' prayers. After spending hours in this remote village near Mount Everest, we returned to Kathmandu.

Exhausted, I lifted my sorrowful pleas to God. Was there any way to reverse what seemed like a final decision?

A local church pastor in Kathmandu had been helping me, and he had an idea—that we would appeal directly to the Home Minister. Only he and the Prime Minister had the authority to reverse the district official's decision.

The big day arrived to meet the Home Minister. We took a taxi to the courthouse, and I waited in the lobby area as my adoption facilitator/pastor went inside the Home Minister's office. Within a few minutes, my friend reappeared, informing me the Home Minister had approved the adoption. I praised God for touching his heart. I had prayed for years to become a mother. Without God's intervention, it never would have happened.

A flurry of activity followed to complete all the paperwork to bring my new daughter back to the States. On one of our many trips through the Himalayan Mountains, I sat in the van with her, waiting on paperwork. The mountains seemed to reach into the Heavens and touch the throne room of God.

It was quiet as the sun arched high in the sky, and the immense beauty around us struck me.

I Corinthians 2:9 came to mind:

"Eye has not seen, nor ear heard,"

I felt caught up to Heaven at that moment anticipating the more excellent eternal home that awaits us. I thought about how there would be no bureaucratic red tape, bribery or endless forms to fill out. I looked forward to seeing God's majesty and splendor that we can only dimly see now. In reflective moments, I've thought about that adoption experience many times.

Recently, however, God revealed something I failed to grasp on that day long ago in Nepal. That vision wasn't just for Heaven—it was for Earth.

I failed to anticipate God's future glory in His Kingdom here—the joy of adopting not one daughter but another daughter from Viet Nam, returning to Nepal two decades later to bring Christian books to a church in Kathmandu, working as a kitchen helper at Echo Bible Camp for kids in Juneau, Alaska; visiting inmates in prison and giving them hundreds of books to read from Christian authors; donating devotional books to an organization helping women caught up in the sex trafficking trade; and even making another trip to Israel.

God had plans for me beyond my wildest imagination. And you also. Have you thought about what Good Works God has prepared for you?

While it's exciting to think about what awaits us on the other side, God gives us gifts and talents to further His Kingdom here. People need the Lord—the rich, the poor, the oppressed, the homeless, the addict, the teacher, the businessman, and the nomads in Africa. The needs are great, and the workers are few.

God gives inspiring examples of people in the Bible who were just like you and me. People no one would have guessed were destined for greatness. Moses was a young baby left in some reed bushes in the Nile River. Joseph was sold into slavery and spent years behind prison walls. Esther was orphaned and hid her identity to protect her adoptive family from persecution. Ruth had no Jewish lineage but became the bloodline of the KING OF KINGS.

These mighty men and women are only a sampling of those God used. They did the most important thing: They loved God and performed Good Works for the Kingdom of God.

We are God's workmanship (Ephesians 2:10). We are His heart in a world becoming more and more godless and more and more corrupt.

> *"Then He said to* them *all, 'If anyone desires to come after Me,*
> *let him deny himself, and take up his cross daily, and*
> *follow Me"*
> *(Luke 9:23).*

The Kingdom of God is here on Earth through His Bible-believing church. We are joined together as One Body through the Holy Spirit to love as Jesus loves us. I John 4:7:

*Beloved, let us love one another, for love is of God; and everyone
who loves is born of God, and knows God. He who does not
love does not know God, for God is love."*

Jesus showed us who He was through His Love and Good Works,
including His death on the cross. When He proclaimed, "It is
finished," He paid for our one-way ticket to Heaven, and Satan was
defeated (John 19:30).

*"Jesus said to him, 'I am the way, the truth, and the life. No one
comes to the Father except through Me'"*
(John 14:6).

What gift has God given you? Use it. What calling has God put on
your heart? Pray about it. What longing keeps you awake at night? Ask
God to fulfill it. What grieves your soul? Ask God what you can do
about it. Don't lose heart. What stirs our hearts stirs the heart of God
even more.

The most important work we can do is share the Kingdom of God
with the lost. Christ's Body, the church, is a formidable weapon that
demons can't destroy, and the Holy Spirit works through imperfect
people like you and me. Ephesians 2:10:

**"For we are His workmanship, created in Christ
Jesus for Good Works** [emphasis mine], which
God prepared beforehand that we should walk in
them."

God's Good Works are unfathomable, His vision is beyond understanding, and our redemption was so expensive only the Son of God
could pay the price.

Don't delay talking to the Savior if you hear God's clarion call. He
will listen if you shout or if you whisper. He is waiting. No bribes,
misfortunes, or sin can hold back the Kingdom of God for those who
love Him.

PRAYER: Please help us, Lord, to pray big. Help us to believe there is no prayer so big that You aren't bigger still.

Chapter Twelve

MOTHERHOOD AND THE TRINITY

"Hope deferred makes the heart sick,
But when *the desire comes,* it is *a tree of life."*
Proverbs 13:12

Motherhood reminds me of the Trinity. I could never be a mother without a child to love. In the same way, only through sacrificial love could God's ultimate Glory be revealed, and that required a relationship with His Beloved Son. And now we are all His adopted sons and daughters through the Holy Spirit: Three in One.

Without children, much of God's love would have dried up in my heart, never to be shared. How much less God's glory would have shone in me?

My daughters would never have known God's love through a young woman, abandoned and rejected; too young to be left childless, too full of promise to be left without Hope, and too hopeful to be left without Joy.

Thank goodness God uses flawed, imperfect human beings. I hate to think how empty my life would be without my two beautiful daughters.

Thank you, Jesus. Thank you, friends and family, who prayed for me every step of the way to Nepal and Vietnam. And I thank our Heavenly Father for adopting us into His forever family. The Kingdom of God is here now, but the Kingdom of Heaven is coming.

PRAYER: Dear Jesus, I pray that You remove abortion from the land. You hold the whole world in Your hands, and that includes the unborn children!

Chapter Thirteen

BLOOM WHERE GOD PLANTS YOU

"And even as they did not like to retain God in their knowledge,
God gave them over to a debased mind, to do those things
which are not fitting;"
Romans 1:28

This spring, I've spent a lot of time gardening. I bought seeds and seedlings and have hydroponics plants and soil plants. Tending to their needs reminds me of God's original garden. Even back then, God needed a gardener.

So He put Adam and Eve in the Garden of Eden, perfected by His Holiness. No weeds grew up, no invaders contaminated it, and no sin possessed it. God made the first humans, created in His image, the caretakers of His perfect garden.

We all know how this story ended when the serpent deceived Eve, and sin became part of human existence. I look forward to the day when God restores His perfect garden. Sin will no longer crouch at the door of my heart, and I won't struggle with doing those things that I don't want to do and not doing the things God created me to do. That is part of our human existence until we enter God's glory.

Sometimes, nature provides spiritual lessons that speak to my heart about the glory of God. I catch glimpses of God in my Earthly garden as I contemplate His future garden in the Kingdom of Heaven.

Recently, I transplanted an orchid that I bought a few years ago. The orchid was not thriving as it could have, and partly out of guilt, I decided to do something to help it enjoy a better life. I'd see blossoming orchids at the nursery and remember my sad orchids just surviving.

I bought soil dedicated to orchids, read about the needs of orchids, put my two plants under a special grow light, and watered them with dedicated orchid food. A few days later, I noticed a lower leaf turning brown and eventually falling off one of my orchids. But I also saw a new leaf popping out, and the appearance of two other healthy leaves had improved.

I thought about my orchid plant. It discarded a "spent" leaf to focus on the still vibrant leaves while using its remaining resources to create a new leaf. Eventually, those healthy leaves will provide the nutrients for the plant to bloom. After all, that's what God created orchids to do—to produce stunning flowers that capture the eyes of the beholder.

I thought about the leaf the plant discarded. In a symbolic sense, am I a discarded leaf, a new leaf, or one being renewed? Can God still use me, or do I risk being pulled up? In the body of Christ, we are either thriving or surviving, and those that are neither—that's a scary place to be. As it says in Romans 1:28:

"...God gave them over to a debased mind..."

As the days become shorter until Jesus' return, we must be busy doing our Father's business. We want to feast on His Word, bloom where God plants us and spread His love to those on the brink of moral depravity. Once that happens, God will no longer invest in their redemption. It's too late for that person, like a dying leaf beyond saving.

Recently, I went to Walmart and bought almost three dozen Dusty Miller plants. Not because I love Dusty Miller plants, but because they were at death's door. They badly needed watering, and I knew I could save them if I took them home. And that's what I did. I planted them, and now they are happy plants. As God's garden caretaker, I rescued them from certain death. A couple of more days, however, and it would have been too late.

We never know how much time we have. We must allow God to be the roots and the vine of our lives. We know our hearts become more rigid the longer we ignore Him. If we wait, it may be too late. Our bad habits become engrained in our everyday living, and sin, always lurking at the door, takes over our thoughts.

In a metaphorical sense, God can remove us in favor of healthier or new leaves. He wants His followers to do more than survive. He wants them to thrive. If we discard those things that hinder us, we can become all God created us to be in this world and store up treasures for His Glory in the next. Feed on the Gardener's Word, soak in His Light, and bloom where God plants you.

PRAYER: Dear Jesus, please help us to feed off Your Word so we can spread the "Good News" while there is still time.

Chapter Fourteen

YOUNG ADULTS AND THE KINGDOM OF GOD

"...whereas you do not know what will happen tomorrow. For
what is your life? It is even a vapor that appears for a little
time and then vanishes away. Instead, you ought to say, 'If
the Lord wills, we shall live and do this or that.' But now
you boast in your arrogance. All such boasting is evil."
James 4:14-16

The young adults' world is different from when I was young, particularly regarding technology. Could it be America's affluence has hindered the desire of young people to read? Why would they want to read books when they have small devices more powerful than the computer that sent man to the moon? Or have we fallen short of giving young adults Good stories to read that glorify God?

I remember going to DisneyWorld with one of my daughters and a friend years ago, and we got into a discussion. My friend said something that caught me off guard. "Why talk about the end times with our kids? Let them live their life, get married, and have a family. They don't want to think about the world coming to an end or the Lord's return."

I didn't respond well to him then because I struggled with that same mindset when I was newly married. My husband was in his second year of medical school. We were watching an HBO pseudo-documentary based on an end-time scenario influenced by the writings of Nostradamus (not the Bible).

While there might be a degree of uncanny accuracy in what writers of that ilk say, they will never be a hundred percent accurate. Anyone who predicts anything that is not one hundred percent accurate is not a prophet of God. Occultists like Nostradamus rely on demonic powers to make predictions, and the Bible tells us not to listen to them. (I didn't know any better at that time).

But I digress. That's not the point I want to make. As I sat and watched the HBO special with my then-husband, I admitted, much to my chagrin, *I don't want Christ to return now. Not after all this work. I want to have children, buy a big house, and enjoy the fruits of what we've labored for.*

That work was arduous labor as a court reporter. I worked long hours in a small town that didn't think women should make more than minimum wage.

I wish I knew then what I know now. And it is this: **We long for the things of this world because we have no idea what better things God has in store for us in the next.**

As the years pass, we fill our hearts with material things. We get married, and our husbands commit adultery. We raise children who rebel. Young people turn from the Lord and go their own way. I know of two Christian families whose sons committed suicide. I know of other Christian families whose children have chosen alternative lifestyles.

We will face adversity sooner or later because we live in the Kingdom of Darkness. The great things we could do for the Kingdom of God take a back seat to live for the here and now. As time passes, sooner or later, we discover that the things of this world that we thought were so great are overvalued and temporary. Whatever the "idol" is that we put before God, it will grow wings and fly away.

However, the struggles of life, in some ways, can be a blessing. Without suffering, we can't become all God created us to be. He made us for so much more. Pain and suffering allow us to turn something meant for evil into good. If we are teachable, we will see beyond this world into the next. We'll realize God didn't create us to live in a fallen world. He created us to live in a perfect one.

Recently, I went to the "Understanding the Times Prophecy Conference" in Minneapolis. As I looked around at the large gathering, I didn't see a single young person. I expected to see at least a couple, perhaps some homeschooling families, but nada, not one.

My friend, long ago, was correct. Most young people will have many years to live before God calls them home, but Jesus could return tomorrow. Death is only a heartbeat away. I want to encourage young people to know Christ personally and live for Him, not themselves.

I won't reveal the final scene in the last book of the *Seventh Dimension Series, The Howling*, but the idea is "to occupy" until Jesus returns. That doesn't mean young people shouldn't get an education, get married, and raise a family, but they should learn how to live for God and live well so they have a testimony to share. They should desire to live in a way that brings glory to our Savior.

Living each day for God until He returns or calls us home is a vastly different mindset than I had that day when my then-husband and I watched that apocalyptic HBO pseudo-documentary. I wanted God to let me live the way I wanted. And, in His infinite wisdom, He did.

I didn't realize then we live in a Kingdom of Darkness, but the life lessons I learned through the suffering I endured weren't wasted. When we suffer for God, God can redeem that suffering and produce Good Works for His Kingdom now and into eternity.

How can we get teens and young adults to realize how quickly time flies? James 4:14 says our lives are merely a vapor, for a little while and then gone. How do we get young people to seize this day, this hour, and even this moment for Jesus?

I've written the *Seventh Dimension Series* to reach those who, like me, love to read. While it's a dwindling number of teens, I believe our future leaders of tomorrow are the young people who read today. A person can't learn all he needs to know to live well only through personal experience.

Reading opens the door to biographies of famous people, traveling to other places, and "tasting" different cultures. For the creative ones, books can take a person to faraway places in time and space, as in the *Seventh Dimension Series*.

Books can teach the reader about God in ways he is unlikely to learn any other way. That's one reason God gave us the Bible, which includes sixty-six books written by many authors who lived and died but died anticipating a better future home. Vicariously, a reader can experience so much more; in my opinion, it can be better than a trip to Disney.

PRAYER: Please help us, Jesus, to stand firm, and when our race is over, to know You used even a lowly servant like me. Thank you, Jesus, that You are returning soon.

Chapter Fifteen

PRISONS OF THE MIND: CAN DEAFNESS SET THE PRISONER FREE

"Who executes justice for the oppressed,
Who gives food to the hungry.
The LORD gives freedom to the prisoners."
Psalm 146:7

Recently a deaf person contacted me, and it profoundly touched my heart. Her struggles are universal, not just confined to those who are hearing-impaired. I pray that my words are thought-provoking and helpful.

Satan's biggest deception is masquerading as an angel of light. He wants to trick us into believing, if it were possible, that Jesus Christ is not the answer. The paradox is that God made us both strong and weak. We are strong in fighting for life at all costs, longing for what He gave us in the beginning. We are weak because we can't find true happiness except in our relationship with Him. If Satan can convince us we can be gods, our pride will make us reluctant to admit we need God. Humility lies at the beginning of the road to salvation.

There are many kinds of prisons, and you've found one of them—the bottle. Prisons null our pain but also take away our freedom—most importantly, the freedom to choose. Similarly, God never takes away our freedom to fail, but He will give us what we need to succeed.

The devil will give you what you think you want, but God will give you Himself. Some prisoners will go to their graves, having sold their souls to the devil. For what? A fabricated lie that will doom them to eternal damnation.

Freedom in Christ will never take away the freedom to choose. If you have made idols of your wants that you believe will bring you happiness, you will be imprisoned in your mind by false gods that can't save your soul. You will have settled for Satan's counterfeit. Sin feels good at the time, but a moment of bliss can bring a lifetime of regret. Ultimately, evil will destroy your ability to hear God's voice. Don't forget that eternity is forever. We will all spend eternity in Heaven or hell. The choice is ours.

You are strong in the sense you have found freedom by conquering your dependency on alcohol. God has blessed you with a spouse to love and cherish. As you have discovered, however, it's not enough to be free FROM something. We need to find our freedom IN something.

Nothing in this world is enough to bring us complete happiness. There are not enough power ball winnings, adoration of fans, cushy jobs, plastic surgery, or computer gadgets to fill our hearts. We weren't made to have a relationship with idols. God created us to have a relationship with Him. God wanted an Earthly human family like He had a Heavenly family. All other pursuits may bring partial or temporary happiness, but they are fleeting at best.

That brings me to the root of your quest for answers. Who is God? You were born deaf, and you have devoted your life to overcoming this limitation to survive in a world where nearly everyone hears. You feel flawed and short-changed, and your perceptions have influenced your choices.

Has it ever occurred to you that God made you that way for a purpose? You might ask, "Why would God do that?"

We tend to ask that question about our "flaws," "disappointments," or "shortcomings." I have asked myself that same question. I've even asked it of others. Why did God take away my friend's eyesight? Why did my beautiful, adopted daughter from Nepal suffer from partial-complex seizures? Why did God allow her to drink contaminated water in Nepal? Why are there 150 million orphans worldwide with little hope of being adopted?

My goal is not to make you feel guilty or to compare your disability with others. You have already done that. We all have. That is part of Satan's ploy to guilt us into feeling like we're no good or trick us into comparing ourselves with others using a legalistic yardstick. God does not measure our value in such a demonic, meaningless way.

We need to remember how much our sin grieves God. It took the death of His Son, Jesus Christ, to make it possible for us to enter the Kingdom of Heaven. Can we truly know the cost of sin in today's Kingdom of Darkness? Do we know the depths of our fallen state without God's divine intervention?

We can't see it—except through suffering. We see affliction when we see a young child die of cancer. We see death on the battlefield. We witness the trauma from a car accident that devastates a family. We mourn when a young person dies from a drug overdose, and we're traumatized when we see the effects of sex trafficking. We shake our fists and proclaim the wickedness of man, aghast that any decent human being could rip out a young girl's genitals and sell her into slavery. We cringe and become angry at what we know is wrong and inhumane.

Our infirmities remind us of our need for Jesus Christ. When we finally realize how weak we are in the spirit to do even one good thing, we'll repent if God is in us. Our blindness, deafness, and diseases awaken us from an indifferent slumber and instill in us a longing for God to wipe away every tear and heal us. We don't suffer in vain—we suffer for God's glory.

If we give our weaknesses to Him, something supernatural happens within us. The Holy Spirit gives us boldness, enabling us to let go of past hurts and forgive. We take our eyes off ourselves and focus our hearts and minds on the One who created us. We remember once again we aren't made for this world. We are made for eternity.

Your ability to rise above your deafness can only take you so far—it can't overcome that emptiness within you that only the Holy Spirit can fill. Jesus Christ is so much bigger than deafness . If you allowed Him into your heart, your heart couldn't contain Him. You would burst with happiness—not because you're deaf, but because your cup would runneth over with joy.

God has given each person many talents. He has given you the gift of writing. If you want God to use you to help others, you must choose one gift you've not yet unwrapped. You need to claim His gift of salvation.

You have figured out how to live in this world marginally happy, but you know something is missing. You're using the freedom God gave you to reject Jesus, His love for you, and His free gift—dying on the cross so you could spend eternity in Heaven.

Forever is a very long time. If you die as a believer, you will be given a new body with perfect hearing in the Kingdom of Heaven. The greatest gift you'll receive in Heaven will be your appreciation for what you never had here. I believe my greatest gift will be the unconditional love of Jesus—the assurance that He'll never leave me.

God manifests His glory in Heaven, but we see glimpses of it here, in the twinkling of the stars against the night sky and in the glistening sand that covers the seashore. If God lavished us with all His gifts here, would we really appreciate them? How many people have died lonely and broken—seemingly, who had everything? How many truly happy people live in Hollywood?

It is out of our need that God fills us. The nothingness is what draws us to Him and enables us to be used by Him. We become His witness, His voice, His legs, His eyes, His ears, and His servants. We become part of the Great Commission.

Ask yourself: How can I use my deafness to draw people into a relationship with Jesus Christ? Use the one thing you don't have to glorify Him—and you will discover your greatest need will become your greatest asset.

Remember, God loves you. He loves you more than you can imagine. Someday you will stand before Heaven's gates. Will they open and allow you to enter? Don't let anyone take away your desire to know the Truth. As the Bible says, the Truth will set you free. The search for answers will lead you down paths only God can answer. You won't find those answers in bottles of wine or quick fixes that lead to death.

I want to share a short excerpt from my book, *Seventh Dimension –*

The Door, about a young girl who spent her whole life bullied and rejected by others. Her worthless and destructive self-image imprisoned her. Read what the King did for her and ask yourself, "Is this not me?"

———

Then the King turned towards me. I now knew the King completely—as my Heavenly Father, the father who loved me, the father who would never leave me or forsake me.

"Your sins are forgiven." He held out his hands, and the fresh scars on his wrists overwhelmed me.

Tears flowed freely.

He said, "I go to prepare a place for you. If I go and prepare a place for you, I will come again and receive you to myself, that where I am, there you may be also."

A birdcage gently floated down from the sky and landed in his outstretched hands. He took the cage and hung it on an olive tree. A small bird sat inside the cage. The King opened the door to the cage, and the small creature walked from its perch and alighted on his finger. He lifted the bird out of the cage, kissed it, and whispered, "You are a daughter of the king."

I realized at that moment he was saying those words to me. I felt his tender kiss on my forehead. I gazed into the sky as the bird flew into the heavens. Before I could say anything, the King was gone.

———

Jesus said in Luke 4:18-19:

> *"The Spirit of the Lord is upon Me,*
> *Because He has anointed Me*
> *To preach the gospel to the poor;*
> *He has sent Me to heal the brokenhearted,*
> *To proclaim liberty to the captives*
> *And recovery of sight to the blind,*
> *To set at liberty those who are oppressed;*

To proclaim the acceptable year of the Lord."

You've been a prisoner long enough. Jesus wants to set you free. He has opened the door to your heart, just as He opened the door to the bird cage for Shale and set her free. Don't delay. Invite Jesus in, ask Him to forgive you, receive the Holy Spirit, and begin the first day of the rest of your life. You have a story to tell that only you can share. Someone needs to hear it, not the least of which is me. I want to know what Jesus has done in your life.

PRAYER: Dear Jesus, I thank you that You've set all the prisoners free—even now and forever.

Chapter Sixteen

A GRATEFUL HEART IN THE KINGDOM OF GOD

"These things I have spoken to you, that in Me, you may have
peace. In the world, you will have tribulation; but be of
good cheer, I have overcome the world."
John 16:33

Can we give thanks in all things? Many years ago, I would have said no. I would ask, "Why did God allow 'this' to happen?"

I was a victim in many situations, including injustices I didn't deserve. I would complain, "If God really loved me, He would fix this or solve that." Or, if I were honest, I would doubt God's faithfulness. "Will He abandon me, too, like my father and husband?"

A thankless heart grieves the Holy Spirit and hurts our relationship with God. Bitterness, anger, and depression will consume us and leave us hopeless.

Gratitude is a strange gift. The more we're thankful, the more we remember things to be thankful for.

One of my most memorable moments of gratitude came in the eighth grade. I lost my notes for a term paper. I didn't know the cards were missing until my last class when the bell rang.

I panicked. I ran down the hall into one classroom after another, checking my desk for the missing notes. Each time when they weren't there, tears welled up. The hours of work I had put into those cards flashed before my eyes, and redoing all that research sickened me. That was when one went to the library to research topics and scoured microfilm and books on shelves.

Inside the last desk I checked, I found my stack of notecards. I wrapped my arms around them and thanked God. Tears flowed—not tears of sadness but tears of joy. I was a straight "A" student, and the thought of those cards being thrown into a trash bin by a janitor was enough to crush me.

Recently, I thought about those three-by-five cards. Much has happened since then. I'm a little grayer, and I imagine a little wiser. I have accumulated many notecards for different term papers.

If we think about it, we're living notes for God's *Book of Remembrance*. God remembers every trial He's put us through, and I dare say each one served a purpose for the Kingdom of Heaven. When we triumph, we earn rewards—or lose them if we fail.

If I'm honest, I would gladly have thrown away some of those notecards through the years. They were about topics I never would have chosen, but God had different plans. My notecards have included lessons about disappointment, heartache, failure, worry, depression, fear, and insecurity. Why couldn't God have given me easier notecards, i.e., how to live like a millionaire? I would have donated lots of money. I could handle that one.

On a more serious note, God's purpose is not to make our lives easier but to prune us to produce fruits for God's Kingdom—love, joy, peace, forbearance, kindness, goodness, faithfulness, gentleness, and self-control.

As the years have passed—and they go by faster the older I get—missing from some of those notecards written long ago is one crucial word—thankfulness. Did I want to thank God for the husband who abandoned me and married his pregnant girlfriend? Did I want to thank God for my barrenness? Did I want to thank God for my twenty years in a profession I hated?

God has taken me down many paths. During most of those years, I did not have a heart of gratitude. I needed to learn something important: Only if I surrendered all my emotional baggage could God use me completely. That included everything I thought served no purpose except to make me miserable.

If we withhold anything from God that needs attention, God can't use us as He would like. We're not able to glorify Him fully; instead, we're busybodies seeking the things of this world and not the things of God.

Look at Hollywood, scan the self-help books on Amazon, listen to the news, and read the newspaper headlines—what blessings can the world give us with its self-centered, I-focused mentality?

I'm thankful God didn't give me all I wanted when I was young. How could God use any of us with a self-seeking, worldly mindset?

I cringe when I think of what kind of a mother I would have been to my kids if God had blessed me with children when I was married. I was a co-dependent, insecure wife seeking all her self-worth from her husband. Talk about dysfunctional in today's psychological terms—I was clueless about what it meant to be a Christian, let alone a Christian wife or mother.

Today, I thank God for the divorce that brought me to my knees. Perhaps I loved my husband more than I loved God. I recommitted my life to Jesus Christ, and God became my husband and provider.

Fatherless as a child opened the door for my stepfather to adopt me when I was ten. His adoption paved the way for a deeper understanding of what it means to be adopted by our Heavenly Father.

My barrenness became a blessing—I adopted two beautiful daughters from Asia, and God is the only one who loves them more than I do.

I could never see the value of my job as a court reporter. How would God use all those words I wrote involving lawsuits without lasting or eternal value? Only when I prayed to God to make me more thankful for the job I hated did God give me something more fulfilling. Those court-reporting skills gave me the foundation for a later career in broadcast captioning, allowing me to work from home while raising my two daughters.

Why didn't God allow me to pursue my dreams of becoming an author? Did He not put those dreams in my heart? Now that my children are adults and I have more time, I can pursue my passion for writing.

When I was young, I looked at the destination, not the process, but it is in the process we grow as image-bearers of God. If the process had no meaning, God could have snapped His fingers and made us perfect. Wouldn't that have been much more efficient and saved time? But God didn't want to do it that way.

Why? It's in the process that we glorify God. What is more beautiful than to see a man or a woman who has overcome adversity give praise to Jesus Christ? We've all seen it—and we watch in amazement.

How easy it is to forget God's passion. He sacrificed His Only Begotten Son, Jesus Christ, so why would God withhold Good from us? There is a mystery in it, but at the center is God. The joy is in the journey and all the opportunities God gives us to glorify Him.

If our attitude toward the hard things glorifies God, we can trust God to help us. As Paul says in Philippians 4:1:

"I can do all things through Christ who strengthens me."

Ultimately, we are most content when we're filled with the Holy Spirit because our true joy can only be found in Him—not this world. Everything else not of God will fade away.

In the struggle, I see God's power. I am like a worm, but God comes alongside me. Often, He's sent friends when I needed encouragement. Scripture instructs me daily, and prayer draws me closer to my loving Father.

I hope to redeem those times of hardship by pointing people to the One who is the Source of all Hope and the Giver of all Joy. Perspective is everything. And when I have a moment of doubt, I remind myself God never wastes anything. Philippians 4:8 says:

"Finally, brethren, whatever things are true, whatever things are noble, whatever things are just, whatever things are pure, whatever things are lovely, whatever things are of good report; if there is anything praiseworthy—meditate on these things."

With a grateful heart, I know God is at work even in the hard things, conforming me into His image. Despite what the devil whispers in my ear or yours, the Kingdom of Darkness can't hide our deeds in the Kingdom of God. The light will shine, and people will see God's Good Works!

PRAYER: Abba Father, please help us not to lose heart. Even though our bodies are wasting away, I pray Your Spirit renews us daily. We know our light afflictions are but for a moment, and they are working in us a far more exceeding eternal weight of glory (II Corinthians 4:16-17).

Chapter Seventeen

WORMS IN THE HEAVENS, THE EARTH, AND THE OCEANS

"But I am *a worm, and no man; A reproach of men, and
despised by the people.*"
Psalm 22:6

Recently some friends and I were discussing when we feel closest to
God. I sheepishly responded I feel closest to God when I am writing
or scuba diving. I feared that didn't make me sound very spiritual—
until someone remarked that's probably when I feel most needy.

I have scuba-dived all over the world, including the Red Sea, the
Great Barrier Reef, and the Caribbean. Thirty minutes from my home
in sunny Central Florida, dozens of cold, clear springs bubble up and
lure divers from around the country to scuba dive in the caves.

On many of these dives, particularly in the Red Sea, away from the
noise and distractions of a busy life, I have been overcome with the
immense beauty and vastness of the world beneath the ocean.

On one night dive in the Florida Keys many years ago, my dive
buddy and I were at about seventy-five feet, which is rather deep for a
night dive. We were diving off a shipwreck, and when I shone my
underwater light on the rustic red side of a sunken boat, I discovered a
brown caterpillar-like creature with tons of legs. He was edging his way

along at a rather slow pace. I probably stunned him with the intrusion of my bright light in what was otherwise total blackness.

As I floated beside the ship and examined the peculiar worm, I wondered why I would be so captivated by this rather ugly creature in the middle of the vast Atlantic Ocean.

I recently had a similar experience with a worm that I discovered in Megiddo, Israel. I stopped to snap a picture, much to the chagrin of my pastor, who later chided me for holding up the bus. Who but someone like me would want a photo of a worm at Megiddo?

Worms are also mentioned in the Bible. One story is about a worm in the Book of Jonah. God sent Jonah to warn the people of the city of Nineveh to repent of their ways. After being eaten by the whale, Jonah traveled to the wicked city and did as God asked him. But when God didn't destroy the city and spared the inhabitants, Jonah brooded over God's mercy to Israel's enemies. Then God supplied a plant to give Jonah some shade as he sat angrily in the hot noonday sun. The next day, however, God provided a worm to eat the plant.

Sometimes life seems like that. God gives. God takes away. Blessed be the name of the Lord.

The Bible references another kind of worm named Wormwood.

> *"Then the third angel sounded: And a great star fell from heaven, burning like a torch, and it fell on a third of the rivers and on the springs of water. The name of the star is Wormwood. A third of the waters became wormwood, and many men died from the water, because it was made bitter"* (Revelation 8:10-11).

Perhaps the most important reference to a worm in the Bible was uttered by Jesus.

> *"But I am a worm, and no man; a reproach of men, and despised by the people"* (Psalm 22:6).
> *"A disciple is not above his teacher"* (Matthew 10:24).

There have been times when I have felt as meaningless as a worm, and bitterness wanted to eat my testimony, like a worm consuming the flesh of the plant. I'm thankful God understands bitterness. But for the grace of God go I.

As my kids get older, I look forward to once again putting on the weight belt, BC, tank, and octopus. I always enjoyed spitting into my face mask to clean it (after all, how many times in life is that acceptable behavior), and, of course, getting that last strand of hair out of the mask so as not to burn my eyes with seeping saltwater. I can't wait to push that regulator button and hear the compressed air spew out (pretty important down there to be able to breathe), and I will waddle like a duck in all my gear to the back of the boat and wait my turn (imagining I look better than I feel with the cumbersome tank on my back).

I will make sure I remember all those hand signals (the out-of-air one might come in handy) and, hopefully, heave off the back of the boat in a spectacular somersault. The rising bubbles as I sink and the sound of the regulator imitating my breathing will bring me back to my favorite pastime. I will be wooed once more to enjoy God's presence in a fabulous world of unparalleled beauty. And for a brief moment, nothing else will matter. Even worms.

PRAYER: Heavenly Father, I am thankful that even though we might be at times as lowly as a worm, You died for us. Someday soon, we will meet in the clouds and be with You forever in Your Heavenly Kingdom.

Chapter Eighteen

BREAST CANCER AND OUR BODIES

*"Or do you not know that your body is the temple of the Holy
Spirit* who is *in you, whom you have from God, and you
are not your own? For you were bought at a price; therefore
glorify God in your body and in your spirit, which are
God's."*
I Corinthians 6:19-20

As someone who has had a double mastectomy and breast
reconstruction for cancer, I have a new appreciation for my body. At
times, I had been critical of myself. Scars from four previous surgeries
reminded me of what I had already endured. While I'm thankful for
the reconstruction, the fake ones are not as good as the real ones.

I could say much more about "imitations"—how Satan gives us fake
peace, fake hope, fake salvation, fake love, and fake truth. Only God
can provide what's authentic. How quickly we forget!

Sometimes, we don't appreciate what we have until we don't have it
anymore, like good health. Cancer steals that from us. I'm thankful to
be cancer-free six years out. I make time for a healthy lifestyle and take
better care of my body, like eating better, getting enough sleep, and
exercising regularly.

The hardest part of my cancer treatment was putting poison (chemotherapy) inside my body.

> *"Or do you not know that your body is the temple of the Holy*
> *Spirit who is in you, whom you have from God, and you*
> *are not your own (I Corinthians 6:19)?*

Taking care of our bodies honors God. We feel stronger spiritually and mentally. We make better choices. We live better, and since we aren't running out of gas, so to speak, pulling ourselves down with negative thoughts and judgmental attitudes, we have more to offer to others. We will love better. We will live out of abundance, not limited by our own needs. We will be a brighter light in the Kingdom of God before Christ returns.

Our bodies are holy, so we should be holy in all our ways (I Corinthians 6:19). When we do that, we will glorify God.

PRAYER: Thank you, Jesus, that we are fearfully and wonderfully made (Psalm 139:14). Help us to honor You by taking care of this Earthly dwelling until we receive our eternal estate in the Kingdom of Heaven.

Chapter Nineteen

I WILL RESTORE TO YOU THE YEARS THE LOCUSTS HAVE EATEN

"So I will restore to you the years that the swarming locust has eaten,
The crawling locust,
The consuming locust,
And the chewing locust,
My great army which I sent among you."
Joel 2:25

"I took away her dreams," my ex-husband told the judge. His words stung. My dreams of bearing children, finishing my college degree, and pursuing my goal of becoming a writer seemed impossible. At thirty, I had hit rock bottom, starting over in a dead-end job I hated. Tears welled up as I wept.

Many decades later, I thank God He did not save my marriage. As an abuse survivor, I learned to be kind to myself. Prayer and reading God's Word helped me to heal. I discovered freedom through travel. I found new ways to obtain my college degree and studied internationally. I eventually earned my Master of Arts in Creative Writing.

I learned to keep a short memory. I overcame bitterness by developing a positive attitude, remembering Matthew 6:33: "But seek first the Kingdom of God and His righteousness, and all these things shall be added to you."

I discovered beauty because I chose to look for it.

> *"Charm is deceptive, and beauty is fleeting; but a woman who fears the LORD is to be praised" (Proverbs 31:30).*

> *I learned to love better. "We love Him because He first loved us" (I John 4:19).*

I adopted two beautiful daughters from Nepal and Vietnam. I homeschooled and learned patience.

> *"Love suffers long and is kind; love does not envy; love does not parade itself, is not puffed up; does not behave rudely, does not seek its own, is not provoked, thinks no evil" (I Corinthians 13:4-5).*

I chose to forgive.

> *"And be kind to one another, tenderhearted, forgiving one another, even as God in Christ forgave you" (Ephesians 4:32).*

I was most surprised to learn that locusts can only eat so much. Then they die.

Learning to be thankful for the little things prepared me for God's generosity in the big things.

> *"...in everything give thanks; for this is the will of God in Christ Jesus for you" (I Thessalonians 5:18).*

Nothing is ever wasted, especially suffering.

> *"For our light affliction, which is but for a moment, is working*

for us a far more exceeding and *eternal weight of glory" (II Corinthians 4:17).*

With God's help, we can share our victories despite our pain.

"He healeth the broken in heart, and bindeth up their wounds" (Psalm 147:3).

God redeems.

"in whom we have redemption through His blood, the forgiveness of sins" (Colossians 1:14).

With the wind at my back and the sand beneath my feet, I no longer lament the years the locusts stole from me. They aren't worth remembering. Only my footprints remain to show where I've been and where I'm going. Hopefully, my walk will encourage others to know they aren't alone.

"And let us consider one another in order to stir up love and good works" (Hebrews 10:24).

PRAYER: Loving Father, help us to follow Your footprints in the sand as we leave our own, forgetting the past and looking forward to the Kingdom of Heaven.

Chapter Twenty

THE HIGHWAY OF HOLINESS

"A highway shall be there, and a road,
And it shall be called the Highway of Holiness.
The unclean shall not pass over it,
But it shall be *for others.*
Whoever walks the road, although a fool,
Shall not go astray,
Nor shall any *ravenous beast go up on it;*
But the redeemed shall walk there,
And the ransomed of the LORD shall return,
And come to Zion with singing,
With everlasting joy on their heads.
They shall obtain joy and gladness,
And sorrow and sighing shall flee away."
Isaiah 35:8-10

Roads have always fascinated me. I often look at them in paintings and wonder about the destination.

When I was married and worked long hours putting my husband through medical school, I had a painting I used to admire while I sat at my desk. A fence was on one side of the unpaved road; overhanging oak trees covered the road on the opposite side. The road disappeared over a mountain and faded into the background.

As I dictated my court reporting notes, I would look at the painting, wishing I could be doing something else. *Where will we live when my husband finishes medical school? What will our lives be like?*

I'm glad I didn't know that road's destination. I wouldn't have wanted to travel it. However, my spiritual journey, or Via Dolorosa, is the best path to the Celestial City God could have given me. It's the problematic roads that mold us or break us; it's the journey that matters. God knows the outcome.

I thank God that, many years later, I'm still here. Some of my friends and family aren't. Everyone takes a different route to the celestial city, but if we love Jesus, we know our destination. Sometimes, people get lost, but those who remain faithful will return to the right path. Some will take the scenic way.

I like what JRR Tolkien wrote in his classic book, *The Lord of the Rings*: "Not all who wander are lost."

While the road I used to ponder was but an old country road, the highway through the celestial city is paved in gold (Revelation 21:21). No more suffering from sin, no more tears shed from broken dreams, no more sorrow to wake up to and no more grieving for what could have been (Revelation 21:4). And, I might add, no more court reporting notes to dictate. Instead, we will shout for joy.

> *"Therefore, if anyone is in Christ, he is a new creation; old things have passed away; behold, all things have become new" (II Corinthians 5:17).*

We are sojourners in a land that's not our home, and when things distract us, cause us to worry, or fill us with anxiousness, let us press on and finish. Good is out there, and it's worth fighting for.

If we follow Your path, even though our efforts might seem paltry, they will not be in vain. We have so much to lose for the Kingdom of God and so much to gain for the Kingdom of Heaven.

PRAYER: Dear Jesus, please help us to stay focused on Your Goodness, remembering Your Goodness is worth every ounce of fight we have, until You call us home.

Chapter Twenty-One

WHAT CAN HOMESCHOOLING TEACH US ABOUT THE KINGDOM OF GOD

"Who is wise and understanding among you? Let him show by good conduct that his works are done in the meekness of wisdom."
James 3:13

Now that my daughters are grown, I look back with nostalgia to our homeschooling years. While some days it was a pleasure and others a chore, I recently thought about our home-schooling curriculum.

In the fourth grade, I gave my older daughter an assignment to set up a study schedule for the week—what subjects and how much time she should devote to each one.

I chuckle as I remember her daily homeschooling curriculum: Reading, five minutes; English, five minutes; science, five minutes; history, three minutes; math, 30 seconds; lunch, one hour; and recess, the rest of the day.

While that might have seemed like an excellent schedule to a ten-year-old, I would hate to imagine where she would be today if I had allowed her to "homeschool" herself without guidance from Mom.

During our homeschooling years, Joy, my younger daughter, and I went to the Florida Homeschooling Convention in Orlando one

Memorial Day weekend. It was a rewarding semi-vacation as I reflected on what we had accomplished over the previous year and what I hoped to do the following year.

Upon arriving, Joy and I quickly ate and hurried down to the exhibit hall, where I pored over books, curriculum, games, and "ideas" on display. Most vendors returned every year, and there were always new ones to check out. This annual tradition encouraged me to continue for another year until God showed me it was time to enroll either of my daughters in traditional school. We took homeschooling one year at a time.

I would assess my daughters' strengths and weaknesses each year and which curriculum (or non-curriculum) would work best for the following year. I didn't use the same materials for each of them. As a homeschooling mom, tailoring the curriculum to meet their individual needs was a joy.

I admit I made mistakes. I tried a math program which caused far too many tears and required the unexpected expense and time of switching to something else. But I never doubted God's calling to homeschool, even as a single parent. At times, I was brought to my knees by the sheer burden and feeling of inadequacy. I couldn't have done it without the Lord's help. He made up for what I lacked.

As I recall what my oldest daughter wanted for a curriculum, in my finite wisdom, of course, I knew one minute of math a day would not prepare her for Algebra. Twenty-five minutes of English a week would not be sufficient to write a term paper on International Relations in college. We can chuckle at the absurdity, laughing because we know ourselves. Are we any different?

In the broader context of life, reflecting on God's plan for us, do I know what my Heavenly Father's perfect curriculum is for me? Do I know what I need in God's economy to become who He created me to be? What would I have chosen if God had asked me to design my curriculum at the beginning of time?

The human side of me would have said, "God, how about a little place on the beach with a pool, lots of books, and a Starbucks latte twice a day? I don't want to cook, wash clothes, worry about car repairs, computers that crash, or anyone I love getting sick. Just give me a life where I never have to worry about anything."

I know it's not very "spiritual," but I don't think anyone would ask for "challenges" if the truth be told. After all, we don't have the mind of God. Our little thoughts are not like His. We long selfishly for a fulfilling life, to have our needs met, and to be accepted by others. The Bible contains all the perils accompanying that mindset, beginning with Adam and Eve.

One of the courses in my life curriculum (which I would have never asked for) was working for twenty years as a court reporter. I never liked court reporting—the adversarial nature of it, the long, unpredictable hours, and the fact that most of what I wrote I perceived as meaningless in God's eternal plan. (Who cares that someone found a cricket in a can of beans?) Plus, I never wanted to do it, but circumstances required it.

Sometimes, life takes away our freedom to choose. In those moments of doubting God's best, it can be hard to keep our eyes on Jesus, who submitted to His Father's will and not His own. I "begrudged" those years until recently, feeling like I contributed nothing to God's Kingdom. How many books could I have written? I can't say discontent consumed me, but on occasion, I have questioned why God didn't allow me to pursue writing at a younger age. Why did "this" have to happen? You can fill in the blank with your "this" and "why."

However, what better choices can there be than what our Heavenly Father's gives us? Do I not trust Him completely? Does He not know the best curriculum to mold me into His image? Cannot my sorrows and loss be counted as joy for the Kingdom of God? And if you look at your life, I imagine you could come to the same conclusion. Jesus tells us in John 15:7:

> *"If you abide in Me and My words abide in you, you will ask what you desire, and it shall be done for you."*

Jesus gave this command to His disciples on the eve of His crucifixion. Little did His followers know what was about to happen. But Jesus knew if His words "abided" within their hearts, it would be sufficient to bring them through the dark days ahead. All of them died as martyrs except John.

We, too, must occupy this Kingdom of Darkness for a while longer, but God has given us everything we need here as sojourners to prepare us for His coming Kingdom. He knitted us together, gave us our talents, and much more. Undoubtedly, His curriculum is vastly better for my soul than anything I would have chosen.

God knows what curriculum we need to complete a doctorate in life and graduate Summa Cum Laude. He lovingly designs the classes, and it will probably require—at least for me—more than 30 seconds of suffering, two minutes of patience, five minutes of sacrifice, and six minutes of prayer.

I suggest if we cease our striving and complaining and slow down to seek God, He might exempt us from a life lesson we would rather not take.

PRAYER: Thank you, Jesus, for Your Good Works in us. Help us not grow weary but magnify Your name in the Kingdom of God.

Chapter Twenty-Two

THE NIGHT IS COMING WHEN NO ONE CAN WORK

"I must work the works of Him who sent Me while it is day;
the *night is coming when no one can work."*
John 9:4

Christians will remember 2020 as the year we celebrated Easter Sunday at home. My House of Worship had its Easter Service on YouTube, and around a hundred other members attended virtually with me. A few hours later, my younger daughter and I ate a home-cooked meal. Then we rested—which is what the Sabbath should be, a day of rest.

The closest semblance to that Easter was when I celebrated Shabbat in Israel in January 1991. That was a few days before the US launched Operation Desert Storm. In stark contrast to the United States, Israel shuts everything down for the Sabbath. Restaurants, shops, and grocery stores are closed, and very few cars are on the road.

Since I finished my cancer treatment, I have come to appreciate how vital a rest day is. I no longer work seven days a week, and even today, I caught myself picking up sticks in the yard and moving a few rocks. God calls that work—and in the Old Testament, God struck down a man for gathering sticks on Shabbat (Numbers 15:32-36). I stopped when God brought to mind I wasn't resting from labor like He wanted me to.

We all struggle with different things, and I tend not to know when to relax. So I appreciated that Easter lockdown when I didn't hear cars zooming by, lawnmowers blaring, or sirens screaming. The neighborhood was quiet, and cars sat in driveways because people were home. Some walked their dogs, and I'm sure many, as I did, spent quality time with family instead of the frenzied pace that marks the way of life for most Americans.

I put on my favorite Christian movie, *The Gospel of John* from 2003, a word-for-word rendering of the fourth Gospel in the New Testament. Every time I watch the reenactment, I come away with a new insight or something God shows me that I hadn't seen before. This time, it was from John 9:4:

> *"I [Jesus] must work the works of Him who sent Me, while it is day;* the *night is coming when no one can work."*

Many people couldn't work during the COVID-19 lockdowns. Schools were closed. Restaurants were shut. All nonessential services, like dry cleaners, barbers, and hair salons, were under lock and key. Sports venues were empty. National parks and beaches were deserted, and theme parks, like DisneyWorld, were vacant. Even places of worship were not allowed to meet in many cities.

To make a point, although it's not my main point, it's worth mentioning because it has never happened in our democracy. When the first case of COVID-19 appeared in China on December 12, 2019, till the World Health Organization declared an end to the public emergency, the world was enveloped in the first global pandemic in over a hundred years. I knew about a coronavirus-like disease in Wuhan from captioning RT News (American media poorly covered it). Still, in my wildest dreams, I never imagined it would grip the entire world or last as long as it did.

The way the United States responded mirrored what happened in most countries worldwide. So much so I felt like I was living in a socialist country and not the US. Our government, at the national, state, and municipal levels, decided what was essential and what wasn't. If you disobeyed the local authorities, you risked huge fines or worse .

Do I even mention the shortages of certain items, like paper towels, toilet paper, and hand disinfectant? Could we have imagined anything like that happening in America? How many times have scoffers laughed at preppers? But here we were: Airports shut down, millions unemployed, and our capitalist system in peril because of an invisible enemy we couldn't see.

During the COVID-19 lockdown, I captioned dozens of breaking news reports and updates at all levels of government, including Trump's first major announcement concerning COVID-19 on Fox News.

While the whole world was affected in a way never before seen, it hits closer to home when your loved one or a dear friend is involved. One of my friends had metastatic lung cancer. Her condition deteriorated during the COVID-19 pandemic, and strict healthcare rules were in effect in Gainesville, Florida.

My good friend had a brain MRI set up to diagnose the progressing paralysis on her left side. She went for her appointment on a hot day in a hot car. When they took her temperature, it was 1/10 degree higher than the acceptable range for incoming patients. They sent her home under the pretense she might have COVID-19.

When she told me, sorrow filled my heart. With only a hundred cases of COVID-19 in Alachua County at that time and a vast medical complex that services the Southeast, the hospital sent my friend home for fear of a virus that had barely touched the area. The authorities deemed the threat of COVID-19 more concerning to the public than my friend's health concerns, which needed immediate care. (And she did not have COVID-19).

I asked her, "Do those people have a brain?" Of course, they have a brain, but they did not consider her increasing paralysis from cancer urgent and sent her home. What an indictment on our medical complex during COVID-19.

COVID-19 brought darkness to our country. People coward at home in fear.

And I don't need to ask, whoever thought a day would come when people wouldn't be allowed to work?

As Jesus said over two thousand years ago, "*The* night is coming when no one can work."

The Bible often uses typology. The Oxford Dictionary defines typology as "the study and interpretation of types and symbols, especially in the Bible."

While the COVID-19 pandemic is officially over, the stage is set for additional fulfillment of this event. We see the "beginning of sorrows" that Jesus spoke of in the Olivet Discourse (Matthew 24:8). He referred to pestilences in Luke 21:10-11:

> *"Nation will rise against nation, and kingdom against kingdom. And there will be great earthquakes in various places, and famines and pestilences; and there will be fearful sights and great signs from heaven."*

When Jesus refers to "kingdom against kingdom," He means the Kingdom of God against the Kingdom of Darkness.

> *"For we do not wrestle against flesh and blood, but against principalities, against powers, against the rulers of the darkness of this age, against spiritual* hosts *of wickedness in the heavenly* places" *(Ephesians 6:12).*

Notice Jesus said, "...fearful sights and great signs from heaven." I don't believe anyone has suggested this might be referring to the rapture. When Jesus ascended into Heaven, His disciples watched Him disappear into the clouds. Imagine what a great sign from Heaven that was. And because of biblical typology, we know Jesus will return in like manner.

COVID-19 was a pestilence and a "fearful sight." As of this writing, in August 2023, according to CDC's website, 1,137,057 people have died from it. What could be more frightening? And many more have suffered debilitating side effects from the disease and the forced vaccines (more on that later).

But getting back to Jesus' words, "I must work the works of Him who sent Me while it is day; *the* night is coming when no one can work," the Holy Spirit impressed upon me what darkness means.

Before COVID-19 struck in the summer of 2019, my daughters and I went on a week-long cruise in the Western Caribbean. We took a shore excursion to Rio Secreto in Playa del Carmen, Mexico. At sixty-four, the trek through the caverns of the underground river was challenging. My daughters handled it easily, but I had to watch my steps using the makeshift cane they gave me.

I thought it would be like a stroll in the park. It wasn't. However, I'm glad I went. After a brief walk through the spectacular rainforest, we came to the underground river's entrance. After forty minutes of climbing over rocks and through fissures in the cave system, we came to a beautiful underground lake. Rio Secreto existed in total darkness for thousands of years before cave explorers discovered it in the early 2000s. The only light was from our helmets and hand-held flashlights.

Then, the guide told us to do something that seemed odd. He asked us to turn off the headlamps and flashlights and lie on our backs in the water. After everyone complied, we created a circular formation, joining hands with the person next to us on both sides. The idea was for us to be at one with nature. The guide took a photo of us in the dark with his flashlight for dramatic effect.

Being one with nature was not what I experienced. I had left my glasses behind in a locker in case I fell. I didn't want to lose the only ones I brought on the cruise. That was probably a mistake. As I lay on my back with the water lapping gently underneath me, staring up at the darkness, I grew nauseated. I tried closing my eyes, but that didn't help.

After what seemed like an eon of time, unbeknownst to me, the lights came back on. I had shut my eyes to shut out the darkness, and when I opened them, I saw several hikers were already standing, and the cave was more lit than dark. I thought my nausea would quickly dissipate when I had light again, but it didn't.

Even when we exited the cave in natural sunlight, my nausea continued. It lasted for an hour or more before finally going away.

I wondered for months why I got so dizzy and nauseous. Then someone said, "It was because you had no sense of spatial awareness."

In everyday language, I didn't have a plumb line. I had no frame of reference in the complete darkness, which made me disoriented and nauseous.

When I think about that experience, more than just the darkness bothered me. I had no sense of anything—up, down, left, right, what was near me, what was far away—nothing.

God did not create us to live in darkness. He is a God of light. Indeed, He is the light. He is our plumb line. When we are in darkness, we are blinded by darkness because we can't see anything, and that makes us sick.

> *"And unless those days were shortened, no flesh would be saved; but for the elect's sake those days will be shortened"* (Matthew 24:22).

Could Jesus be referring to another darkness that's coming when people won't be able to work? Or was He referring to the night we experienced during COVID-19?

The COVID-19 pandemic plunged us into darkness—including COVID-19's origins, and the mandated protocols left many people emotionally damaged. I still see some folks walking around wearing face masks in September 2023. We also will never know how much COVID-19 curtailed the spreading of the Gospel. Missionaries were sent home from their assignments for a year or more.

How many people quit going to church? How many lived in solitary confinement for months, unable to visit loved ones in hospitals or attend weddings and funerals? How many of us watched videos of people screaming through apartment windows in China because they were shut up without food and starving?

The COVID-19 pandemic may be prescient of a longer-lasting darkness when things will be much more severe than what we just endured. It's easy to miss the flip side of Jesus' words. If the days are shortened, the nights are longer. To quote John 9:4 again, Jesus said:

"I must work the works of Him who sent Me while it is day;
the night is coming when no one can work."

Based on Scripture, I have no doubt the day is coming when we won't be able to witness or share Jesus Christ with the lost or do the works of the Lord. God brings to mind the word "occupy." We don't know how much time we have before the Lord's return, but we are to occupy and be busy doing His work, as Jesus said.

Many Christians do not believe in a rapture or think it comes at the midway point or the end of the Tribulation. In my opinion, the rapture could occur several years before the seven-year Tribulation begins. The Bible says it happens when it's not expected.

"Therefore you also be ready, for the Son of Man is coming at an
hour you do not expect" (Matthew 24:44).

If you think about what Jesus is saying, He's not referring to when He returns to set up the Kingdom of Heaven. We know that day once the Antichrist confirms the treaty with Israel (See Daniel 9:27). The seven-year countdown begins at that point, the final week allotted for Israel. Jesus returns at the end of that 70th week to begin His millennial reign. That means we would also know the midpoint of the Tribulation.

"But of that day and hour no one knows, not even the angels in
Heaven, nor the Son, but only the Father" (Mark 13:32).

Until that day, we must be about our Father's business, sharing the Gospel and doing all we can to fulfill the Great Commission.

If you haven't accepted Jesus Christ as your Savior, today is the day of salvation. When night comes, it may be too late. You may not be able to get on the Internet. You may not be able to work. You might not even have food to eat. John 3:16 says:

"For God so loved the world that He gave His only begotten

Son, that whoever believes in Him should not perish but have everlasting life."

God's light shines out of the darkness; that is our plumb line in these last days. May God be glorified as we seek to be His servants. Let us work while we still can. Let us shine for Jesus unto salvation as long as we're here.

PRAYER: Dear Jesus, please let Your light shine brightly in us so people will want to know You before the Great and Terrible Day of the Lord.

Chapter Twenty-Three

MOSES SPOKE OF THE RESURRECTION

"Now see that I, even I, am He,
And there is no God besides Me;
I kill and I make alive;
I wound and I heal:
Nor is there any who can deliver from My hand.
For I raise My hand to heaven,
And say, 'As I live forever."
Deuteronomy 32:39-40

"Rejoice, O Gentiles, with His people;
For He will avenge the blood of His servants,
And render vengeance to His adversaries;
He will provide atonement for His land and His people."
Deuteronomy 32:43

Have you wondered if there is a reference in the Old Testament to the death and resurrection of Jesus Christ? While researching time reversals in the Bible for *Seventh Dimension - The Howling*, I came across these two passages: Deuteronomy, 32:39-40 and 32:43 (see above).

I also found this fascinating article on the web: *Resurrection, Reversing Time & DOD Monitoring Here.*[1]

The original piece suggested how God reversed the sun's position by ten degrees in the Bible, referring to Ahaz's sundial:

> *"'Behold, I will bring the shadow on the sundial, which has gone down with the sun on the sundial of Ahaz, ten degrees backward.' So the sun returned ten degrees on the dial by which it had gone down" (Isaiah 38:8).*

Since then, the author has updated it with even more compelling information, like explaining the "death and resurrection" process as a time reversal.

Most of the information the author presents is out of my comfort zone; I'm not a mathematician, but the reference to Deuteronomy is enlightening. Even in the Old Testament, God gives hints about a coming resurrection.

In Deuteronomy 32:43, Moses alludes to His return as the Messiah, to avenge the blood of His servants, render vengeance on His adversaries, but He would be merciful unto His land and His people.

Jesus said to the scribes and Pharisees shortly before His crucifixion:

> *"See! Your house is left to you desolate; for I say to you, you shall see Me no more till you say, 'Blessed is He who comes in the name of the LORD!'" (Matthew 23:39).*

As we near the days of the Tribulation, I'm always looking for passages in the Old Testament relevant to the Messiah's return, particularly in the Torah.

Interestingly, these Deuteronomy passages also infer no one can take away those God has called. Yeshua lifted His hands on the cross (death), and His human life was swallowed up in victory (eternal life).

While time reversals may be scientifically possible, I would hate to trust my eternal destiny to a human hypothesis. God can and has reversed time in the past, but believing He will give us a second chance, a third chance, or a fourth chance in the future is risky business.

Each time we say no to God, we harden our hearts. How many opportunities do you need to do what you can do today? A day is coming when God will not delay His return, run the clock backward, or reverse time. The Kingdom of God is here; today is the day of salvation. Don't delay if you haven't accepted Jesus as your Lord and Savior.

PRAYER: Please show us, Abba Father, how to reveal Yeshua Hamashiach to the Jews.

Chapter Twenty-Four

THERE SHALL BE TWO MEN IN ONE BED

"I tell you, in that night there shall be two men in one bed; one will be taken and the other will be left."
Luke 17:34

I recently read Luke 17:34 and needed to think about it. Why did I not remember reading that verse before? Something seemed unnatural to me about it. When has it been "normal" for two men to sleep in one bed? Could the passage signify another sign of the end times—that it would be natural for men to have unnatural sleeping relations?

Jesus' words disturbed me so much I went to a King James Bible published in the late 1800s to ensure the passage read the same way. To see God's unchanging Word from a Bible over a hundred years old reminded me no matter how much things around us change, God's Word is unchanging.

In the last days, God has promised to reveal Himself to those who are wise. When Jesus came the first time, He physically opened the eyes of the blind and shut the eyes of those who refused to receive Him—the lost sheep of Israel. As Jesus' return nears, those with the Holy Spirit will discern the signs of the times. God will open their eyes.

Recently, I watched a YouTube video, and a pastor made the same observation—he did not remember that verbiage. He wondered if it could be because of the Mandela effect—an event where many people incorrectly remember something from the past in the same way.

Perhaps people had misremembered the verse. However, if God's Word is unchanging, it must be because God has opened the eyes of the discerning.

As of 2015, all fifty states allowed same-sex marriage in the United States. The boundaries between right and wrong and pure and profane have become blurred. In the Scriptures, profane usually refers to unnatural sexual relations. II Peter 3:3-4 says:

> *"...knowing this first: that scoffers will come in the last days, walking according to their own lusts, and saying, 'Where is the promise of His coming? For since the fathers fell asleep, all things continue as* they were *from the beginning of creation.'"*

The question becomes, if two homosexual men are in one bed and God takes one man and leaves the other, why would God take one and not the other? There must be something else in this passage Jesus is inferring. II Corinthians 5:21 says:

> *"For He made Him [Jesus] who knew no sin to be sin for us, that we might become the righteousness of God in Him [Jesus]."*

Luke 17:34 (referenced above) gives much insight into the dystopian world before Jesus returns. One man is taken, and the other is left. Hidden in Jesus' words is homosexuality is not the unpardonable sin.

Jesus' shed blood frees us from the bondage of homosexuality and many other sins the Bible says will be rampant in the last days.

I always remember the more profound my sin, the more excellent the opportunity for God to show His amazing grace to me—and the same grace is available to all who repent and ask for forgiveness.

PRAYER: Abba Father, we know perilous times are coming, and homosexuality will be rampant in the last days. Even though it is not the unpardonable sin, please help us not to fall into that temptation or any temptation, but deliver us from evil, for Thine is the Kingdom, the Power, and the Glory, forever.

Chapter Twenty-Five

SOCIALISM AND THE KINGDOM OF GOD

"Behold, I [Jesus] send you out as sheep in the midst of wolves.
Therefore be wise as serpents and harmless as doves."
Matthew 10:16

———

When an economics class insisted that socialism worked because it was a great equalizer, the professor followed up by saying, "Okay. We'll have an experiment. I'll average the grades, and everyone will receive the same grade. No one fails, but no one receives an "A."

After the first test, the professor averaged the grades, and everyone got a B. The students who studied hard were upset, and those who studied little were happy.

As the second test rolled around, the students who studied little studied even less, and the ones who studied hard previously decided they wanted a free ride, too, so they studied only a little.

The second test average was a D!

No one was happy.

When the third test rolled around, the average was an F.

The scores never increased as bickering, blame, and name-calling all resulted in hard feelings.

To everyone's great surprise, all failed. The professor told them, "Socialism would also ultimately fail because when the reward is great, the effort to succeed is great, but when the government takes all the reward away, no one cares enough to succeed for the benefit of someone else.

———

The above story, quoted from several Internet sources, may be spurious, but it's an interesting analysis on the mechanics of socialism. None of us are so Godly and self-sacrificing we are willing to work our behinds off for the State's welfare without regard to our personal sacrifice and the cost to ourselves.

And neither is it biblical.

> *"For even when we were with you, we commanded you this: If anyone will not work, neither shall he eat" (II Thessalonians 3:10).*

Socialism takes away the hard work ethic Americans historically have been known for and equalizes available resources for "the good of all."

Socialism runs counter to Christian beliefs because the government takes away the individual's freedom and ability to choose, and what's "good for all" is forced on society by a godless government.

The government, for example, is not wise enough to decide what's best for my family, and when they rob me to give what is rightfully mine to someone else, most of the surplus ends up in the pockets of those who least deserve it.

In the Parable of the Ten Virgins, found in Matthew 25:1-13, the five young virgins who brought extra containers of oil for their lamps were not "forced" to share with those who didn't. Why? Because there would not have been enough "capital" or oil available to care for everyone who came to meet the bridegroom.

The five virgins without sufficient oil were not disabled—they could talk, walk, think, and reason. Implied in the context is they could care for themselves. Jesus called them "unwise." The wise virgins instructed them to "go to those who sell oil and buy some for yourselves."

Implicit in the story is a free market economy where resources are available, implying the foolish virgins could have bought some earlier but didn't.

The foolish maidens preferred to depend on handouts from the wise who had planned, much like many today are looking for the government to take care of them in the form of bailouts for fiscal mismanagement; free money for cars, houses, and education; entitlements for government welfare; funding social issues like abortion; and free health insurance that could bankrupt our country.

Jesus admonished us to help the poor, saying they would always be with us, the thought being no matter what a nation does to equalize wealth, it goes counter to God's natural law.

Everyone is not guaranteed the ability to own a home, have health insurance, or whatever else our government decides should be funded by those with more. The government will end up robbing its citizens to pay for what is not affordable.

Socialism is not sustainable because fewer and fewer will be able to survive economically at a high enough level to provide for those who are unwilling. The government will dupe many into thinking they can't make it to validate their desire for ultimate control. The whole system will collapse under its waste of mishandled resources and broken dreams.

Too many young people believe they are entitled to "more." Someone insisted in response to my arguments on Facebook, "The government is going to take care of me."

Good luck with that. The problem is somebody has to pay. Ultimately, we all pay because we all suffer when people experiencing poverty suffer, and there will be many more who are truly poor.

When limited resources are squandered by propping up those who deserve to fail and the government uses available capital to equalize all there is, everyone suffers. We see this now and will see more of it because we're currently using money that doesn't exist.

The future earnings of our children, borrowed money from other countries, fiat money created by our government, Social Security, and probably, eventually, our retirement accounts, will be used to fund our government's fiscal irresponsibility. There will be a continued shrinking of the private sector as the government takes over more and more of the economy. A day of reckoning is coming.

God said in the end times, He would send a strong delusion. I see a lack of discernment everywhere, sadly, most of all in our young people. Too many have bought into the lies fed to them by the educational system and powerful bureaucrats in Washington. I blame both the Democrats and the Republicans. In many ways, I hardly see a difference between them except on the issue of abortion.

Do they not know our nation's history or is it easier to believe the delusion than to seek the Truth? Even Pontius Pilate, who represented the mighty Roman government, asked, "What is truth?" as Jesus Christ stood before him. The question I ask is, do you know?

I implore you to seek the Truth in Jesus Christ if you don't know Him as your personal Savior. Who knows when the last bastion of freedom will be taken from us.

In China, the government filters much of the news. The Google search engines remove "propaganda" the government doesn't want the masses to know.

Christians are imprisoned and martyred in Russia, South Korea, and Vietnam for speaking the truth. In Europe, Islam is the fastest-growing ethnic minority, and Sharia law is becoming the norm. Muslims make it no secret what their agenda is through their attacks on our country, faith, and way of life.

The CCP is making inroads and will do anything to jeopardize our sovereignty. The WHO wants all the countries in the world to cede authority to them. It's not about freedom. It's about power. How long are we going to be in denial for the sake of political correctness?

While the government in 2008 might have thought Freddie Mac, Fannie Mae, AIG, and others were "too big to fail," perhaps today nobody realizes the free United States in 2023 is not too big to fail. It is not even in question.

A reader chastised me for using this parable in this context. My response is it's a biblical typology for the Lord's return and a statement on how we should live our lives. I originally wrote this piece in the early 2000s, and it's more relevant today than when I wrote it.

If we have any clue about what's happening in the financial sector, CBDCs (Central Bank Digital Currency) is just around the corner. The government can't wait to put its mark on our hard-earned money and tell us how to live.

China's model is coming to America. We are a nation in bankruptcy, and this is how we'll come out of it—smelling like a skunk. The foundation for the implementation of CBDCs is worse than socialism. It's communism.

The Bible says Jesus will rapture His Bride in the blink of an eye, so wake up, or you might miss the bridegroom. Spread the Good News in the midst of all the bad. And pray for wisdom. Remember, God is for us.

I will share a personal story as an addendum to this piece to make an important point.

I stored gold coins in a depository with a couple thousand other depositors worldwide. Last fall, when one customer could not retrieve his funds from the vault, the government froze the assets, and the "powers that be" performed an audit. The law firm handling that part of the case initially said there could be as much as $80 million missing. The last I heard, the missing funds totaled over $120 million.

Where did that gold and silver go? If you have that much money hidden, all you have to do is share a couple of million to hush people up, then go to jail for a few years, and when you get out (maybe even early), you're a wealthy man.

My point is this: Don't trust anyone with whatever God has given you. Don't trust the banks (they are going to fail). Don't trust your neighbor. Don't trust your financial advisor. We live in an age of deceit, the Kingdom of Darkness. We live in a world Jesus describes vividly in Matthew 24-25. Why did Jesus tell us so much about the end times, and why did the Apostle John write an entire book (Revelation) about future events?

God has forewarned us, so we are without excuse. There is no reason we should be the five virgins running out of oil. While the

Kingdom of God is here, we need to be "wise as serpents and harmless as doves (Matthew 10:16)." Why would I give my gold to a stranger and pay him to store it for me? I was foolish. But a wolf won't fool me again.

The IRA rules might allow the government to seize IRA accounts after implementing the CBDC system. In *The Coming Economic Earthquake*, Larry Burkett said this many years ago.

I want to emphasize this point. Many people think their retirement funds are secure in a bank vault. However, when the government implements the Central Bank Digital Currency, the government will have access to your money. For all intents and purposes, the government will "own" it.

The Kingdom of Darkness is infiltrating our religious, political, social, economic, judicial, climate, and food production. The Kingdom of God won't be here as a restrainer when the church is gone. The Holy Spirit will be, to some degree, probably similar to His appearance in the Old Testament, but the hardness of men's hearts will make the Holy Spirit's presence scarce. The world will run amok with wild men and desperate women trying to survive the judgment of a just and righteous God.

My advice: Don't wait until after the rapture to accept Jesus into your heart. The Kingdom of God might only be here for a short while longer. Once God removes the church, the world will be so dark that survival will be a constant struggle.

Take heart, though. Jesus will return, leading the charge on a White horse followed by His bride and Kingdom warriors.

Don't leave Earth without securing your ticket to Heaven. It's a no-return ticket, bought and paid for by Jesus. Today is the day of salvation. Don't wait.

PRAYER: Our heavenly Father, please help us to be as wise as serpents and harmless as doves. Everything we own belongs to You, and we have the Holy Spirit within us and are sealed for the day of redemption.

Chapter Twenty-Six

SINGLE PARENTING – 16 NUGGETS OF WISDOM

"Train up a child in the way he should go,
And when he is old he will not depart from it."
Proverbs 22:6

Recently, a friend shared with me her daughter was in the process of adopting two children. The little girls had been abused in their family of origin, and the legal case was slowly making its way through the courts. As I reread her email, I prayed God would answer every prayer my friend's daughter sent up, just as He had answered mine.

Then the thought occurred to me: What would I say to a young mother-to-be whom God has called to "walk in my shoes"? I know each person's situation is a little different, but similar in that a woman feels God is leading her to single parent an orphan, an abused child, or a child who might never have felt loved. What wisdom would I impart after being at this noble but difficult task for almost thirty years?

I pulled out my keyboard, and a plethora of thoughts gushed forth.

I hope my "words of wisdom" will encourage you if God has chosen you to adopt an orphan—whether you are married or unmarried, especially if you are single. With God, all impossible things are possible. Without Him, we walk alone.

———

1. Single parenting is the hardest thing you will ever do but the most rewarding thing you will ever do.

2. I would never recommend a single woman adopt. It's too hard. I would never recommend a single woman not adopt. The blessings are too great. Allow God to tell you what to do. If God calls you to adopt, never back down, give up, despair, or listen to those who tell you differently. Nothing can prevent you from being a mother to a child if God is in it. God has a plan and a purpose. He does things His way, not ours. Trust in God. He will direct you.

3. You will never know what tired is until you have single-parented two kids alone (or even one).

4. God is your husband and the perfect husband.

5. You will understand how much God loves you when you adopt a child with no future and no hope. That is how we are without Jesus.

6. You will share the heart of God, His hands, His hope, and His "all" with your children. They will know God through your sacrificial love.

7. You will love more than you ever thought you could, and you will fail miserably. But your children will love you anyway. Acknowledge your mistakes and move on. God will shine through your shortcomings. He loves your children more than you do.

8. God will not abandon you. He will meet every need you have more abundantly than you can imagine.

9. The day you sign the adoption papers will be the best day of your life. God has given you a great gift—a chance to share His love with an orphan, the essence of our faith.

10. "Mommy" is the most beautiful word in English.

11. Enjoy every moment of the journey. Your children will grow up too fast—in the blink of an eye. The years will wiz by and you will wonder where the time went.

12. Make the most of every opportunity to love, teach, laugh, cry, and even be silly. Be a mother to the fullest. Give it your all. Go to bed exhausted. It's the best kind of tiredness you'll ever feel.

13. Have a latte every once in a while, and read your Bible every day. On days when you can't, know God loves you anyway.

14. Pray hard. God is always with you. Know this is your calling and your life's work. Your children are precious gifts from the Hands of the Creator. They are beautifully designed in His image with a future and hope because of your love freely given in His name.

15. Love your children unconditionally. Be flexible. Learn to say, "I'm sorry." It does wonders to restore the hurting soul.

16. Enjoy the journey and have a blast. There is nothing else like it short of eternity!

———

PRAYER: Dear Jesus, I thank you for my two beautiful daughters. I wouldn't have my Children of Dreams if it weren't for You.

Chapter Twenty-Seven

COUNTERFEITS AND GOOD WORKS

"In this you greatly rejoice, though now for a little while, if need be, you have been grieved by various trials, that the genuineness of your faith, being *much more precious than gold that perishes, though it is tested by fire, may be found to praise, honor, and glory at the revelation of Jesus Christ."*
I Peter 1:6-7

———

In the classic movie *The Wizard of Oz,* following a tornado, Dorothy's house deposits her in the land of Oz. Longing to find her way back home, she is encouraged by the good witch, Glenda, to follow the yellow brick road. "The mysterious wizard might be able to help you return home," she told Dorothy.

Dorothy sets off on the yellow brick road toward Emerald City and meets three friends. Their trip is interrupted, however, by evil witches who bring darkness to the fabled land.

Eventually, Dorothy discovers the disappointing truth. The wizard who was supposed to help her return home is a counterfeit. Her dog, Toto, exposes him as a fraud.

———

Here is another fabled story that crossed my path.

———

A man tried to sell a one-ounce Maple Leaf on a beach in a prominent section of town. "Will you buy this gold coin for $50?"

"No, I don't have any money."

He approached a woman. "Would you like this Canadian coin for only $25?

"No."

"Why not?"

"I don't have $25."

"Suppose I offer this to you for free. Will you take it?"

The woman turned it over and examined it. "It's beautiful."

"Do you want it?"

"No."

———

Beachgoers didn't want the gold coin because they only knew the counterfeit—green paperbacks.

A look at history might reveal a clue about this stunning revelation. Gold, a precious metal, has been used by man since ancient times for commerce. Long ago, people recognized it for what it was—rare and valuable; but today, passersby can't even identify genuine gold on a beach.

During the Great Depression, governments around the world abandoned the gold standard. In 1933, Congress and President Roosevelt banned private ownership of gold and asked citizens to turn in their gold at $35 per troy ounce, essentially robbing Americans of their wealth.

Although it became legal to own it again in the 1970s, the money changers (Federal Reserve Bank and central banks) suppressed its value to bolster the dollar and manipulated the system to their advantage.

Gold became worth less than counterfeit because it was not considered a currency, thus enabling the Federal Reserve and the central banks to control the vast money supply.

Counterfeit "gods" mark the last days. Sports enthusiasts go to sports events to numb their pain. Hollywood fans idolize Hollywood stars, wondering what it would be like to be rich and famous. Small-minded people think this "idol" or "diversion" will make them happy, and there are many "wicked wizards" who want to manipulate the masses with fear and deception so they can "own" them.

While *The Wizard of Oz* is only a story, it symbolizes our longing for home. We meet all sorts of people along the way, and the evil one tries to derail us. But God's messengers help us to make it safely home.

In Heaven, nothing is counterfeit, and we will behold all the Good Works of God. Jesus will welcome us on a magnificent road paved in gold. And as beautiful as I imagine that road will be, what I long to see most is my Lord and Savior. All the gold in the universe can't purchase that first-class, one-way ticket to Heaven.

PRAYER: Dear Jesus, please help us not to love the counterfeits of this world here today and gone tomorrow. May our faith be more precious than gold when tested by fire. May we bring praise, honor, and glory to Your name.

Chapter Twenty-Eight

QUE SERA, SERA; WHAT WILL BE, WILL BE

*"And if I [Jesus] go and prepare a place for you, I will come
again and receive you to Myself; that where I am, there you
may be also."*
John 14:3

If I were a betting woman, I'd make two predictions. I won't win a
million dollars in the lottery since I don't play, and I won't be the first
female president of the United States. My older daughter used to tell
me I'd make an excellent president—before I became dumb during her
teenage years. Fortunately, I have become smart again since she turned
twenty-one.

Now, I get to be dumb again as my second daughter enters that age
of smartness. At least I know what to expect the second time around.
Admittedly, I look forward to the day I'm smart again unless dementia
sets in. We won't talk about that.

When I was nine, one of my favorite songs was *Que Sera, Sera; Whatever Will Be Will Be*. That was when I believed anything was possible.
However, my child-like dreams did not include all the injustices of
living in a fallen world.

We're closer to God in our youth—before sin strips away our innocence. Kids easily believe in miracles or magic. Call it what you want. No wonder when we're old, we must become like little children. Are we redeemed enough to see our Savior through the shattered glass of broken dreams? A child sees the glory of a risen King—and asks no questions. Older people see the King through difficult circumstances—and ask too many.

In retrospect, I am thankful God did not give me most of the things I wanted. He gave me what I needed. God's gifts don't always come wrapped in pretty boxes. They arrive in more mysterious ways. Sometimes, it takes time to see His inner workings, and that's tough for impatient people like me.

It would have been much easier to go to a store and pick up a book on *How to Get Your Life Straightened Out*, *Fix Your Broken Marriage*, or *How Not To Be Dumb During the Teenage Years*. If I could follow a twelve-step program to fix Lorilyn Roberts (never mind everybody else), I'd read that book in a weekend. Come Monday morning, I'd have my act together. That would be so efficient. So, like me.

God knew better. He knew I needed time. Only time would grow me into the Christian woman He desired me to be. And only time will develop you into the Christian saint He wants you to be.

Only where wisdom seeded itself would understanding be revealed —to write my soul's passions and feel God's Spirit through my words. God knew I longed for children. Only He knew how to make that happen (Lord knows I tried). Isaiah 55:8 says:

> *"For My thoughts* are *not your thoughts, nor* are *your ways My ways," says the LORD.*

Someday, I hope to understand what that means. It's one of those "mysteries" that God will explain to me—if I still wonder after seeing His scarred hands and feet.

When I was married, shortly before my husband left, I read the above passage and implored God, "Oh, please, let not your ways include divorce." I became paranoid. I trusted a husband who had been unfaithful to me more than I trusted my Heavenly Father who died for me. I feared the ridicule of my family and church and the whispers.

The ugly wounds from childhood would bite me once again. Was I not even good enough to keep a husband?

Now I chuckle. I may not be good enough for the most mundane task on any given day. I have learned to laugh at myself—even when I am the only one laughing. My daughters will tell you.

I remember time is fleeting, pain is temporary, and the future is extraordinary. So I peck away at the keyboard, confident that I won't go to jail for not filing my taxes—I just finished them today—and I'm glad to live another day. Why? So I can get out of bed in the morning, go to work, and pay more taxes.

I will remember to feed the dogs in the evening (or they will yelp), set the air conditioner to 77 when I go to bed (or I will sweat), and fill up the car with gas—it's always empty. I won't speed down 39th Avenue where that female police officer lurks behind a sign (I would know), and I will get my half-and-half at Publix so my coffee will taste almost as good as Starbucks. I am still working hard to kick that habit.

If your life is like mine, most of it boils down to the mundane, the ridiculous, and the absurd. Without my Lord and Savior, my passion to write would be squelched by the tyranny of the urgent, and I think I'd go insane. God's voice within me removes the edge, lowers my blood pressure, and convicts me of the essentials. He reminds me to pray for those who are hurting, and I delight in His Word—and wonder why I fail to read the Bible more often.

Or maybe I'll curl up on the sofa with my Kindle and get lost in a book begging to be read—and write reviews for authors who wait with baited breath. I would know that, too.

I'd fail to find Goodness in the land of the living without my relationship with Jesus Christ. His Spirit brings me hope—for my daughters to marry Christian men and have a passel of kids; for my future—to live into my 90s like my grandparents; and for forgiveness for my past sins—even the ones I don't remember.

God gives me the drive to live life to the fullest—work hard, play hard, and not sweat the small stuff. If the small stuff trips me up, I remind myself I will never run out of stories. My Border Collie knows all about my tripping, and he lived to tell about it.

Regrets—don't play that game. You will never glimpse your marvelous future if you keep looking back.

We have an awesome God who is preparing a place for us so where He is, we can be with Him.

> *"But he who is joined to the Lord is one spirit* with *Him"* (I
> *Corinthians 6:17).*

In that day, we'll shine with His light in our glorious bodies with no more wrinkles, gray hair, and fat bellies. Que sera, sera; whatever will be, will be, and it will be far grander than our eyes can see.

PRAYER: Dear Jesus, please help us to love You more today than we did yesterday. Help us to love You tomorrow more than we do today. And please help us to remember that while life is fleeting, opportunities abound to do Good Works in Your name. And when we lie down, we will say, "Que Sera, Sera; whatever will be will be."

Chapter Twenty-Nine

THE MASTER BUILDER AT WORK

*"He [God] has made everything beautiful in its time. Also He
has put eternity in their hearts, except that no one can find
out the work that God does from beginning to end."*
Ecclesiastes 3:11

Joy, my younger daughter, and I stood before the glass artisan,
anticipating his newest creation. The old, bearded man picked up a
small, clear glass tube with callused hands and gently stroked the form-
less shape. The two-thousand-degree fire spewed from the dragon's
mouth, and we could feel the intense heat from a few feet away. While
others came to the medieval fair for entertainment and sports, we
came to enjoy the musicians and artists.

Would he create a dog, a cat, a dolphin, or something else from the
dozens on display? Hundreds of discarded glass shards were scattered
about on the table. If the broken pieces had been found elsewhere,
someone would have thrown them in the trash.

But in the hands of an expert, little creatures of beauty sprang
forth. The man "knew" his creations before he sculpted them. He held
the object to the flames as we stood transfixed, wondering what would
emerge.

Unable to bear the suspense any longer, my daughter asked, "What are you making?"

The glass artisan glanced at Joy with a look of satisfaction. "I'm making a hummingbird."

Hidden in the worthless shards of glass was beauty. A tiny bird with flapping wings, a high tail, and a long beak emerged from the cylindrical shape. The intricate creation looked like the little winged creature that visited our red hummingbird feeder in the summer. It was hard to believe something so delicate could be forged from the hot flames.

Watching the artist create beauty with such passion reminded me of the Creator who created the world out of nothing. God flung the stars into the darkness to form light. He shook the Heavens to release droplets that blanketed the Earth, filling the valleys with abundance. He carved the mountains as monuments that stretched into the sky. Everything God created was good.

> *"Then God said, 'Let Us make man in Our image, according to Our likeness'" (Genesis 1:26);*

When God finished His work on the sixth day, He described everything as "very good."

Even after humanity's fall, God created beauty by devising a plan to rescue us. Despite the messes we make, God sees what we can become.

When we're afraid, He loves us. When we fail, He provides another way. When we're sick, He heals us. When we're discouraged, He comforts us. When we sin, He redeems us. God has a plan when we don't have a clue.

Even in our fallen state, the imperfections that mark us as sinners can't conceal God's image within us. God knows us better than we know ourselves. He promises hope, love, peace, and more.

Our Heavenly Father wants to have a relationship with us and gives us opportunities to serve Him. If we listen, we can hear His voice—never more than a heartbeat away. May we seize those intimate moments God gives us and not forsake our first love. Even if we fail,

God will not abandon us. There is no condemnation, and we're never alone (Romans 8:1).

God is the Author who penned the most extraordinary story ever written. He is the Artisan who formed the Heavens and the Earth. His Son is our Savior, and as we near the end of the church age, Jesus is preparing mansions for us so we can be with Him forever (John 14:2-3).

Just as the artisan envisioned his creation out of the broken shards of glass, the Master Artisan sees through the brokenness of our lives. He heals us and makes us new. As I contemplate the Wedding Feast, I remember, I'm the bride of the King and, therefore, royalty in the Kingdom of Heaven.

> *"And I heard, as I were, the voice of a great multitude, the sound of many waters and the sound of mighty thunderings, saying, 'Alleluia! For the Lord God Omnipotent reigns! Let us be glad and rejoice and give Him glory, for the marriage of the Lamb has come, and His wife has made herself ready.' And to her, it was granted to be arrayed in fine linen, clean and bright, for the fine linen is the righteous acts of the saints"*
> *Revelation 19:6-8.*

Today, the hummingbird sits on a shelf in all its beauty. I hope God will marvel at me someday, just as the artisan held up the hummingbird and nodded his approval. It would be wonderful to hear our Savior say, "Well done, my good and faithful servant."

PRAYER: Thank you, Jesus, for making everything perfect in its time. Eternity beckons us to keep on keeping on, knowing You created us for Good Works. May You receive all the glory and honor for the Good in us.

Chapter Thirty

KINGDOM AGAINST KINGDOM

"And for this reason, God will send them strong delusion, that they should believe the lie."
II Thessalonians 2:11

When I began writing *Seventh Dimension - The City*, the fourth book in the *Seventh Dimension Series*, God wanted me to show the battle between Jesus Christ and Satan. I didn't want to write about the Powers of Darkness. I prefer not to think about Satan, the occult, and demons because, to be truthful, those things scare me.

I had been exposed to some occult practices when I was young (a friend talking to demons on a walk through the woods and séances in middle school). I even had someone give me an Ouija board as a gift. I tossed the board into the outside trash bin and stayed as far away from those things as possible.

I asked God why He wanted me to write about spiritual warfare because the first three books in my *Seventh Dimension Series* are historical, and I heard Him say in my head, "Because the occult won't tempt you."

I knew nothing about that world beyond those experiences I had early in my life, so in my head, I said, I will learn what I need to know and write the book as quickly as possible. *Seventh Dimension – The City* is the fastest book I've written to date—and, I might add, the easiest.

While writing that book, I learned something important. For the last fifty-plus years, I've lived a comfortable Christianity. Not that my Christian walk has been easy, and not that I haven't endured trials and hardships. But compared to the Tribulation on the horizon, I'm hesitant to characterize anything about my Christian walk as hard.

When I look at Iran, Israel, Syria, Ukraine, China, Sudan, Korea, France, Taiwan, Ethiopia, Lebanon, Russia, and other countries, civil unrest and wars are rampant. Jesus said in Matthew 24:6:

> *"And you will hear of wars and rumors of wars. See that you are not troubled, for all* these things *must come to pass, but the end is not yet."*

The West will not go gently into the night before the Lord's return. The days ahead for America look bleak. We are ignorant to think we'll escape suffering even if we don't experience the wrath of God.

> *"And Jesus answered and said to them, 'Take heed that no one deceives you'"*
> *(Matthew 24:4).*

> *"And for this reason, God will send them strong delusion, that they should believe the lie"*
> *(II Thessalonians 2:11).*

Could I be deceived? Could you be deceived? Matthew 24:7:

> *"Jesus said, 'For nation will rise against nation, and kingdom against kingdom. And there will be famines, pestilences, and earthquakes in various places.'"*

"Kingdom against kingdom" is the Kingdom of Darkness battling the Kingdom of God. After the final battle in Jerusalem, when Jesus defeats Satan and his minions, Jesus will begin His reign as KING OF

KINGS and LORD OF LORDS. Think about what we pray when we say the Lord's prayer:

> *"Our Father in heaven,*
> *Hallowed be Your name.*
> *Your kingdom come,*
> *Your will be done*
> *On earth as it is in heaven.*
> *Give us this day our daily bread.*
> *And forgive us our debts,*
> *As we forgive our debtors.*
> *And do not lead us into temptation,*
> *But deliver us from the evil one.*
> *For Yours is the kingdom, the power, and the glory forever.*
> *Amen"*
> *(Matthew 6:9-13).*

Satan offered Jesus an opportunity to avoid the cross by giving Him all the world's kingdoms if He [Jesus] would bow down and worship him [Satan] (Matthew 4:8-9). Jesus did not succumb to Satan's temptation even after fasting forty days and forty nights in the wilderness.

In the last days, the Kingdom of Darkness will stage their troops and equipment in the valley of Megiddo as they gather for the greatest battle in history. That final conflagration will take place in Jerusalem. Until that time, we must remember the "prince of the power of the air" rules the Kingdom of Darkness by proxy, but the devil has not been given Jerusalem, and he does not control it.

Jesus did not fall for Satan's temptation. I don't know if I've shared this in the past, but if you look at the cover of *Seventh Dimension – The City*, you will see a rocky land devoid of life. If it were possible for Jesus to have succumbed to the devil's temptation, the book cover depicts what the world would have become—a barren wilderness.

Satan's rule from Jerusalem would have followed the death of every human being because Jesus would not have gone to the cross to save us. I don't think we can fully appreciate what it cost Jesus to give us eternal life.

That's why the "abomination of desolation," spoken of by Daniel the prophet and referred to by Jesus is so crucial. Jesus said in Matthew 24:15-17:

> *"Therefore when you see the* abomination of desolation,
> *spoken of by Daniel the prophet, standing in the holy place"*
> *(whoever reads, let him understand), "then let those who are*
> *in Judea flee to the mountains."*

The abomination of desolation marks the beginning of Satan's three-and-a-half-year reign called the Great Tribulation.

In 1998, when my older daughter experienced an epileptic seizure, the cause was nearly impossible to diagnose based on ambiguous MRIs. It was called a "zebra" in medical jargon. We went to Yale University so a renowned pediatric infectious disease doctor could examine her. This physician was the only one who was confident my daughter had a "worm in her head," known as neurocysticercosis.

She assured me it was treatable, that my daughter would fully recover, and she did not have what was initially labeled a brain tumor. Her expertise reassured me, and I traveled to Vietnam a week later to adopt my second daughter.

How could this doctor be so sure of the diagnosis despite the doubts of others? How could she give me that assurance? Because she knew what neurocysticercosis was. She was one of the leading authorities on the condition in 1998.

Do we know the times in which we live? Have we studied Scripture and asked God to open our eyes? Are we ready for the bridegroom's return like the five wise virgins in the Parable of the Ten Virgins (Matthew 25:1-13)? Or are we like the five foolish virgins who missed the wedding?

I've always been struck by what Jesus said in this parable:

> *"And the foolish said to the wise, 'Give us some of your oil; for*
> *our lamps are going out.' But the wise answered, saying,*
> *'No, lest there should not be enough for us and you; but go*

rather to those who sell, and buy for yourselves"'(Matthew 25:8-9).

The wise virgins did not (or perhaps could not) give their oil (the Holy Spirit) to the foolish virgins.

A few years following the health crisis of my daughter, I wrote an article about the experience. I explained how she contracted a parasite in Nepal before I adopted her at age 3. I wrote the article to warn other adoptive parents about neurocysticercosis. I didn't want anyone else to bring home an adopted son or daughter and deal with the uncertainty and fear I had faced, something that could easily be remedied with a simple deworming pill—just like you give to dogs and cats and farm animals for hookworm and other parasites.

After publishing the article, the producers of Animal Planet's *Monsters Inside Me* contacted me. They had found my blog post and wanted to feature our story.

A few years after the airing of the episode, one of the producers emailed me and asked if I knew of anyone else who had adopted a child and had a similar story of a parasitic infection. I told her one person had contacted me and said he was "filled with worms and didn't know what to do."

The producer said the person had Morgellons syndrome. Of course, I had no idea what that was, so I searched the Internet. Someone suffering from Morgellons syndrome believes he is infected with parasites.

The producer of *Monsters Inside Me* could tell the difference between someone with an actual parasitic infection and someone who thought they had one and didn't.

Do I have that perception regarding current events and what the Bible says about end-time events? Do I know God's truth well enough to tell a fake story from a lie or a delusion? Luke 21:26 says:

> *"...men's hearts failing them for fear and the expectation of those things which are coming on the earth, for the powers of Heaven will be shaken."*

Until recently, I couldn't imagine what could be so horrific that men's hearts would fail them. What could be worse than a nuclear bomb? While that is scary, it would not cause my heart to die, as Jesus describes. Could it be because I've lived with the possibility all my life?

I believe some things will be worse than that—supernatural things. Luke 17:26 says:

> *"And as it was in the days of Noah, so it will be also in the days of the Son of man."*

When I think of these words, I imagine people living in sin, forgetting God, and living a lifestyle consumed with wickedness. II Timothy 4:3 describes people in the last days as having "itching ears." But I think Jesus was hinting at something more sinister than human wickedness. What was different about the time of Noah?

If you are anything like me, you might have sat in a church pew for the last fifty years and never heard about the Nephilim. You might never even have heard about trans-humanism and the creation of hybrids. I would be surprised if you heard it from the pulpit.

Are you familiar with CERN, located on the border between France and Switzerland, and its mission? Look at its logo. Doesn't it look like the number 666? Why is there a statue of Shiva, the Hindu God of destruction, at the entrance to the facility? And if you aren't familiar with it, you probably don't know they built the complex on top of an ancient pagan temple of Apollyon.

Few pastors would have the courage to address controversial topics like UFOs, UAPs (unidentified aerial phenomenon), alien abductions, and animal mutilations. I was impressed Pastor Jack Hibbs gave a two-part sermon on UAPs from Calvary Chapel in Chino Hills, California.

Congress recently had a hearing concerning UAPs, and it's been trending in the news. If you are anything like me, I'm sure you would rather listen to a Godly pastor speak on these things than a reporter who gets his script from a news organization censoring the truth.

Perhaps even more disturbing is the relationship of the Vatican with the Mount Graham International Observatory. Of all the nicknames they could have given the telescope, they named it Lucifer. What is the Vatican looking for in the skies?

How many know about HAARP, the High-Frequency Active Auroral Research Program in Gakona, Alaska? The former military-funded research site was connected with the University of Alaska in Fairbanks until 2015 when ownership was switched to the University of Alaska Fairbanks. Could the program be linked to chemtrails? Conspiracy theorists say the US government is spraying metallic toxins into the atmosphere. Why would they do that?

I have mentioned only a few things here to show you why knowing God's truth is essential and why we need to be informed and prepared for the last days—whenever those days come. We don't know God's timetable, but there are signs. We also don't know the day or the hour when the rapture will happen.

I believe the only thing holding back "the time of Jacob's trouble" is God's merciful hope that people will turn to Him and repent. As a nation, we have a lot for which to repent.

When I originally wrote this article, the Pope was making a historic speech to the US Congress (September 24, 2015). Pope Francis is the only Pope ever to address a joint session of Congress. When I think about what has happened since 2015, my words resonate with more truth today than when I originally wrote them. Back then, these topics were fringe. The Powers of Darkness are no longer hiding their agenda.

Since 2015, climate change has become a religion, not just a concern of a few liberals. While once taboo, marriage between two people of the same sex is culturally acceptable. Censorship in America is becoming commonplace. Government intrusion into our lives through forced vaccines, school shutdowns, restriction of travel, and mask mandates have forever changed the American psyche. The repercussions will be felt for years.

More recently, many unexplainable things have happened, like the burning of Lahaina on the island of Maui. Things don't add up—almost like it was intentional, but why?

God is allowing Satan to have his way for a time, but the Kingdom of Darkness will not last forever.

I remember my ability not to be deceived comes from the Holy Spirit and reading God's Word: The Bible. We risk deception if we minimize what Satan can do. He knows his craft well, and he knows his time is short. He has plenty of minions roaming the Earth looking for bodies to possess. Have nothing to do with these "masqueraders of light."

We live in the Kingdom of Darkness, and deception is rampant. Who are some of those deceived people? They are reporters and news anchors. They are judges, lawyers, doctors, professors, scientists, and teachers. They serve in the halls of Congress in Washington DC. They are actors in Hollywood. They are famous sports icons. They are authors and musicians. They are rich and poor. They are the power brokers and the money changers, including the elite and the Illuminati. Anyone pushing for a New World Order is part of Satan's grand deceptive scheme. These influential people include those who practice freemasonry, worship Satan, and even those who claim to be Christians but aren't. We must remember Ephesians 6:17-18:

> *"And take the helmet of salvation, and the sword of the Spirit, which is the word of God; praying always with all prayer and supplication in the Spirit, being watchful to this end with all perseverance and supplication for all the saints—"*

> *"God has not given us a spirit of fear, but of power and of love and of a sound mind"*
> *(II Timothy 1:7).*

Will you get the jitters if the stock market crashes a thousand points this week? Do you have some cash stashed away for a few months or even longer if the banks fail? Do you have a few weeks of food set aside if panic-driven mobs empty the shelves at the grocery store? What if there is no money at the teller machine because our country is in a financial meltdown and no cash or credit is available?

CBDCs are coming, and if you research what they are, you will know Central Bank Digital Currency is evil. Anytime a government can control the money of its people, it will. Social credit scores are also coming, just like in China.

In simple terms, what it means is if you don't do what the "prince of the power of the air" says through his human agents, you'll be shut down. You will be denied access to your money, experience food rationing, be scandalized, and, eventually, perhaps thrown into prison. What is the catchphrase we've all heard repeatedly, coined by Danish politician Ida Auken and later attributed to the World Economic Forum in 2016? "You'll own nothing and be happy." If you want something, you'll rent it, and it'll be delivered by drone.

I could continue with other scenarios. What if the power grid fails and your house turns dark? Are you prepared for that kind of adversity? It could happen. It's happened before.

More importantly, are you ready to suffer if the rapture doesn't happen until much later? Are you prepared to die for your faith? A friend of mine who has a friend whose husband is a trucker pulled into a truck-weighing station on the highway. When they checked the contents inside his truck, they found guillotines. Why would anyone be transporting guillotines in America?

We live in uncertain times. My most significant concern is for the Church. We expect lost and deceived people to do unrighteous things, like advocating abortion. But I have Christian friends who believe if a woman wants to kill her baby in the womb, it's her right.

We need to stand for truth when it comes to marriage. Don't cave in, and don't compromise. God made man and woman to come together and procreate through marriage. To believe anything other than this is an abomination. Don't be deceived.

We could be on the verge of the greatest Christian awakening in history, but I don't think it will come until God raptures a couple of billion people. After that happens—and it could be a short period or longer—the final week of the seventy weeks, as prophesied in the Book of Daniel, will happen.

In biblical terms, one week equals seven years; Christians call it the Tribulation. In Jeremiah 30:7, that time is described as "...the time of Jacob's trouble..." Jacob refers to Israel.

Take heed; God isn't done with the Jews. Replacement theology, where people believe the Church has replaced Israel, is another lie perpetrated by Satan. If God doesn't keep His promises to the Jews and Israel, what guarantee do we have He'll keep His promise to us, the Church?

God mercifully brought the Jews back to Israel in disbelief. That's why they need us more than ever—to witness to them. The Kingdom of God is here in the hearts of true believers. It is here by way of the Holy Spirit. God has not abandoned the Jews.

On the contrary, Jesus will judge which nations enter the Kingdom of Heaven based on how they treated the Jews during Jacob's trouble—the Tribulation. If we won't be a friend to the Jews and Israel's protector now, why would we do so during that time?

Accepting the Mark of the Beast instead of believing in Jesus as the Son of God will cost Earth-dwellers (those left behind following the rapture) their life. The dispensation of Grace (Church age) is over when God raptures the Church. The Earth-dwellers will fight for their lives every second of every hour. Revelation 12:11 says:

> *"...they overcame him [the antichrist] by the blood of the Lamb and by the word of their testimony, and they did not love their lives to the death."*

I don't believe we are prepared physically, emotionally, or spiritually for what's coming. We are too complacent sitting in front of our television screens, filling our already too-full bellies with ice cream and snapping silly selfies with our latest iPhones. I am also guilty, but trying to do my part to alert others—God needs you. He needs you to be a witness.

Christians need the sleeping church to wake up from its laziness.

> *"For we are His workmanship, created in Christ Jesus for good works, which God prepared beforehand that we should walk in them" (Ephesians 2:10).*

The Holy Spirit enables us each day to perform Good Works for the Kingdom of God, but do we do it regularly?

We must begin with a repentant heart. We must seek God's forgiveness for the greatest holocaust since World War II—the killing of the unborn child. Their blood cries out for justice. We should shake in our shoes over God's coming judgment—not only for murdering babies in our country but for setting a precedent for the rest of the world. We have led the whole world astray.

We have sacrificed our children at the altar of convenience and, ultimately, Satan's altar. We have fed the false religions of this world with the blood they crave—just like the heathen in ancient times. Don't be deceived. There is power in that blood—the power of life. Don't believe for a second God has turned a blind eye to the one billion plus children aborted worldwide. Judgment is coming.

Pray for our country. Pray for our children. Pray for revival. Pray for the peace of Jerusalem. Pray no matter what happens, we will not waiver in our faith, whether we see demons coming in UFOs who claim to be our saviors or our country is invaded with strange apparitions that are part human and part demonic (Nephilim). We will not take the Mark of the Beast. We will die for our belief that Jesus Christ is the KING OF KINGS and LORD OF LORDS. We must remember who wins. The battle belongs to the Lord (I Samuel 17:47), who will give us the strength and grace to do His Good Works until He returns.

Remember: Good is present in the Kingdom of Darkness. We are sojourners, and the Good here is worth fighting for. God does not want anyone to perish. Repent and turn to God. Pray—in the car, in the shower, in bed, and at work. Pray unceasingly.

> *" The effective, fervent prayer of a righteous man avails much"*
> *(James 5:16b).*

PRAYER: Dear Jesus, please let us not be deceived. May Your Word be so engrained in our hearts and minds that we will see Your truth and long for Your blessed appearance.

Chapter Thirty-One

THE CODE OF LIFE: DEBUNKING OF EVOLUTION

*"Every good gift and every perfect gift is from above, and comes
down from the Father of lights, with whom there is no variation or shadow of turning."*
James 1:17

Can we trust Jesus as our Savior and accept the evolutionist's view that
the first living cell evolved from a primordial mix of gases?

If we believe God gives us life after death, why is it a stretch to
think God breathed life into us in the beginning? Imagining a concoc-
tion of gases spontaneously combusting into something called life
seems illogical. Imagining molecules with enough intelligence to evolve
into a higher form seems even more skeptical. If that were true, why
don't the "building blocks" continue to develop into a super-human
race?

Is not our belief that God "created man" in Genesis 1:27 as
compelling as Romans 8:11:

*"And if the Spirit of Him who raised Jesus from the dead is
living in you, He who raised Christ from the dead will also*

give life to your mortal bodies through his Spirit, who lives in you."

> *"Who is this who darkens counsel*
> *By words without knowledge"*
> *(Job 38:2)?*

As lofty as the evolutionist's ideas, his words are without knowledge. Even with all the great discoveries since Aristotle and the advancements in genetics, scientists cannot create DNA. John 1:1 adds:

> *"In the beginning was the Word, and the Word was with God, and the Word was God."*

Not only is matter and energy needed to create life, but knowledge is essential.

Every living creature's code of life is hidden, even in a tiny one-celled organism. It is so intricately complicated that we cannot replicate it. Nature possesses the mystery of life, but it was given to it by the Creator.

Just as God will bless us (or damn us) with eternal life after we die, God gives us life here. Can a person accept Christ as his personal Savior and believe he has evolved from a lower life form? The concept seems contradictory and would ridicule God's creation story in Genesis.

I envision the theory of evolution going the way of the dinosaurs. Science evolves, and knowledge increases, but the Bible is unchanging. God's Word is the same yesterday, today, and tomorrow. And I take comfort some things don't change. My beliefs are embodied in the cornerstone of salvation, not the whims of science. Science doesn't have the answers to the creation story and cannot prove anything—except its own inconsistencies.

PRAYER: Thank you, Jesus, there is no shadow or turning with Thee. You are the same yesterday, today, and tomorrow, and Your Kingdom is an everlasting one. A Kingdom without end.

Chapter Thirty-Two

DIVERSITY AND THE UNITY OF CHRIST

"For you are all sons of God through faith in Christ Jesus. For as
many of you as were baptized into Christ have put on
Christ. There is neither Jew nor Greek, there is neither
slave nor free, there is neither male nor female; for you are
all one in Christ Jesus. And if you are Christ's, then you are
Abraham's seed, and heirs according to the promise."
Galatians 3:26-29

While the media tries to make us think diversity will strengthen our country and help us be more tolerant, the contrary is true. When diversity is used to show differences between people, it divides them.

On 9/11, when our nation was attacked, the people of New York came together in an unprecedented way. It didn't matter if you were black, white, wealthy, or poor; people wanted to help each other because they were hurting.

In the Middle East, differences in race and ethnicity keep people apart. Often, diversity does not draw people together; it divides them.

In Christ, we are one in the spirit. We are all part of God's family. Whenever I meet a fellow Christian, whether I am in Florida, Asia, or

Australia, everything else about the person takes a backseat. I know we're one in Christ and I'm speaking to a brother or sister in Christ.

No country has ever survived when diversity was emphasized over the unity of the people. As we stray farther and farther away from the Judeo-Christian principles on which our country was founded, it's only a matter of time before "diversity" undermines enough of the fabric of our country that we can no longer stand.

No longer united as "One Nation Under God," what will we become? God made us all unique and special, but we are part of one body—the body of Christ. Once we elevate diversity above unity, we risk catastrophic consequences. In Luke 11:17, Jesus said:

> *"Every kingdom divided against itself is brought to desolation, and a house* divided *against a house falls."*

Jesus Christ is the most divisive person who ever lived. He separated the believers from the unbelievers, and His divisiveness confounded the leaders of His day. But the unity of the believers became the cornerstone of His church.

Can we see harmony and diversity through God's eyes as Jesus did 2,000 years ago? He knew men's hearts and what was in a man. That is the challenge set before us. May God grant us the ability to see diversity in the unity of Christ.

PRAYER: Heavenly Father, we are Yours, sons of God. We are Yours, the seed of Abraham. We are Yours, heirs, according to the promise. We are Yours, born again into the Kingdom of Heaven. We are Yours, sealed by the Holy Spirit.

Chapter Thirty-Three

THE FOOL SAYS THERE IS NO GOD

"The fool has said in his heart,
'There is no God.'
They are corrupt,
They have done abominable works,
There is none who does good."

"The LORD looks down from heaven upon the children of men,
To see if there are any who understand, who seek God.
They have all turned aside,
They have together become corrupt;
There is none who does good,
No, not one."

"Have all the workers of iniquity no knowledge,
Who eat up my people as they eat bread,
And do not call on the LORD?
There they are in great fear,
For God is with the generation of the righteous.
You shame the counsel of the poor,
But the Lord is his refuge."

"Oh, that the salvation of Israel would come out of Zion!
When the Lord brings back the captivity of His people,
Let Jacob rejoice and Israel be glad."

Psalm 14

After finishing my breast cancer treatment in December 2017, I committed to reading through the Bible each year.

Three months into my new adventure, I discovered many surprises. I was farther along in my walk with God than when I read through the Bible years earlier, and I was spiritually in a different place. Things I'd read previously without understanding leaped from the pages, and I found unfamiliar passages rich with meaning.

I was in the habit of only reading my favorite passages. I discovered a vast treasure trove of books, stories, and life lessons I never knew or didn't remember. How exciting it was to see the things God was showing me. More recently, I've been "reading" through the Bible each day by listening to the Bible.

In Psalm 14, I used to wonder what it meant when it said, "They have all turned aside. Together they have become corrupt. *There is* none who does good,"

Is that true? Does no one do good? Perhaps putting it into the context of a timeline, Psalm 14 is apocalyptic. Maybe it's referring to the Tribulation when God's people have been removed or put into a protective place, and the Earth-dwellers who remain are wicked and corrupt.

We know in the future, salvation will come to the Jews. Isn't it amazing that God predicted the salvation of His covenant people?

> *David cried to God: "Oh, that the salvation of Israel would*
> *   come out of Zion!*
> *When the LORD brings back the captivity of His people,*
> *Let Jacob rejoice, and Israel be glad"*
> *(Psalm 14:7).*

I'm amazed that God restored the Jews to their land in unbelief on May 14, 1948. Of course, the complete restoration of the Jews to their promised homeland won't happen until God establishes His Kingdom here on Earth and Yeshua reigns as KING OF KINGS and LORD OF LORDS.

> *"'And it shall come to pass in all the land,'*
> *Says the Lord,*
> *'That two-thirds in it shall be cut off and die,*
> *'But one-third shall be left in it:*
> *'I will bring the one-third through the fire,*
> *'Will refine them as silver is refined,*
> *'And test them as gold is tested.*
> *'They will call on My name,*
> *'And I will answer them.'*
> *I will say, 'This is My people';*
> *And each one will say, 'The LORD is my God'"*
> *(Zechariah 13:8-9).*

Because my salvation experience began in elementary school with some Jewish classmates, I've always been passionate about reaching the Jews for Jesus. Many Jews seek Him, especially the mystics, because they read the signs and know the Scriptures. But they don't realize it's His second coming, not His first, that's on the horizon.

I also believe percentage-wise, more Jews will be saved than Gentiles in the last days. One-third of Israel, the Bible says, will come to know Yeshua as the Messiah shortly before He returns as KING OF KINGS. From what Psalm 14 states, it might be an even smaller percentage of Gentiles.

The fool says in his heart, "There is no God." How many times have unbelievers mocked Christians? As the Tribulation nears, anti-semitism and Christian censorship will increase. During the seven years of "Jacob's Trouble," most Earth-dwellers will be unbelieving fools.

These scoundrels will be living in fear and corrupt in every way. Their works will be abominable, and there will be no one who does good. At that time, people on the Earth will be so wicked that God says they will "eat up my people as they eat bread."

The Bible hints that things will get so bad and food such a rare commodity people will commit cannibalism to survive.

But "God *is* with the generation of the righteous." At no time has God abandoned those who love Him. The Jews will have a place prepared for them by God where they will be safe from harm—if they accept Jesus as their Messiah and escape to Petra before the Antichrist and his minions slaughter them.

God has spoken two things to me: Be bold and share the Gospel. A sense of urgency speaks to my heart. I hope readers will be encouraged to read the Bible each day, remembering God has something to say to each of us. Oh, that we would crave to hear His voice!

> *"Do not harden your hearts as in the rebellion,*
> *In the day of trial in the wilderness"*
> *(Hebrews 3:8) .*

PRAYER: As the world becomes increasingly darker, please keep our hearts tender and love You more. Please help us not to grow weary in doing Good.

PART 2

Tales to Ponder

"When the whole world is running towards a cliff, he who is running in the opposite direction appears to have lost his mind."

-CS Lewis

Chapter Thirty-Four

BLACK LIVES MATTER – CHRISTIAN FRIEND OR FOE

"There is neither Jew nor Greek, there is neither slave nor free, there is neither male nor female; for you are all one in Christ Jesus."
Galatians 3:28

———

The round clock at the front of the classroom struck 9:00 a.m. Sunlight streamed through the whitewash blinds and fell on my wooden desk. I clasped the newly sharpened pencil. Did I dare look to the back of the room?

I bit my lip as I studied the kids around me. The girls wore brand-new dresses, and the boys were in their Sunday best. I knew boys didn't care how they looked—except the first day of school.

I glanced at the calendar—August 28, 1966. Today was my first day of fifth grade and the beginning of a new school year, a new classroom, and many new faces. However, it wasn't like any other first day of school.

I eyed my new teacher sitting at her desk. Why didn't she introduce the new students seated in the back? I supposed that would be awkward. To point out those in the back would only draw attention to them. They weren't like us white kids—or so I was told.

I stole a glance despite my conscience telling me I should quit peeking. I was bothered by everyone ignoring the new kids. The room was tranquil. I could only hear whispers. No laughter. No warm greetings. No jokes. Just—whispers.

I turned to look into the eyes of one of the black girls. Could I read fear on her face? Could I sense shyness in her unwillingness to make eye contact? Or was it something else?

In a classroom of uncertainty and scorn, I knew what it was like to be different. Long-buried memories resurfaced, and I felt their discomfort, alone in a sea of white faces.

———

The above story introduced me to desegregation in fifth grade in Cobb County, Georgia, north of Atlanta. Much progress toward racial equality has been made in the years following. However, I fear the Black Lives Matter Movement (and later the Woke Agenda) threatens to undermine what's been achieved. The founders spearheading the campaign have added an underlying goal unrelated to the core issue.

I'm not going to minimize the problem of prejudice and racism. I know it exists, but I genuinely believe it's a people problem, not a nation one. If one looks hard at America compared to other countries, racial equality is more the norm here than anywhere else. We are a vibrant culture—mainly due to the number of immigrants. The truth is, except for the Indians, we are all immigrants.

For a moment, though, I want to focus on African Americans. On May 25, 2020, I was as disturbed as everyone else to witness the murder of George Floyd at the hands of three white Minneapolis police officers. What happened was pure evil. Regardless of what preceded such an atrocity, to hold a helpless man down on the ground for almost nine minutes and stand by and watch his life slip away was inhumane.

It makes me wonder if those police officers were psychopaths. I hope the legal system punishes them to the fullest extent of the law. In my mind, they should receive the death penalty. But this is where I draw the line: Because three officers in Minneapolis used poor judgment, it cannot be used as a basis to judge all police officers.

One cannot use one injustice (killing George Floyd) to fix other wrongs (e.g., defunding the police), which would have a disastrous effect on society. To riot, set buildings on fire, create autonomous zones where police are forbidden to go, or embrace and give credence to a movement like Black Lives Matter is only perpetuating evil.

I captioned the local Santa Monica news when rioters were stealing and robbing from stores. The police stood by and did nothing. I am a single mother, and I found this appalling. It made me consider that I needed to arm myself and know how to shoot like a pro.

And that's what I did. I bought a gun and took a course on how to use it. Who knows when I might have to defend myself or my daughters because the police can't or won't. We live in dangerous times. If we continue on this path, we will have anarchy.

Is that justice? What are people thinking when they say they want to defund the police? Look at what happened in Seattle's Chaz Zone (Capitol Hill Autonomous Zone). The area was off-limits to Seattle police. There were two shootings within forty-eight hours. One person was killed, and another was critically injured.

I captioned Fox News when rioters destroyed businesses in the Chaz Zone, and the police did nothing. Who knows how many rapes and assaults took place. I want to give these people the benefit of the doubt. Perhaps they are well-intentioned, but they are sorely misguided to come up with this ill-conceived solution. One person is needlessly dead, and another is critically injured.

These demonstrators, encouraged by "Black Lives Matter," have exchanged God's moral law or standard for one based on a tribe's governing rules. Whatever the tribe says is right. If you have a different set of standards, you're part of the problem. That makes what's right and what's wrong morally relative. What does that create—lawlessness. In Matthew 24:10-12, Jesus told his disciples when the end of all things would be:

> *"And then many will be offended, will betray one another, and*
> *will hate one another. Then many false prophets will rise up*
> *and deceive many. And because lawlessness will abound, the*
> *love of many will grow cold."*

In II Thessalonians 2:6-8, the Apostle Paul wrote to the church:

> *"And now you know what is restraining, that he may be revealed in his own time. For the mystery of lawlessness is already at work; only He who now restrains will do so until He is taken out of the way. And the lawless one will be revealed, whom the Lord will consume with the breath of His mouth and destroy with the brightness of His coming.*
> *"The coming of the lawless one is according to the working of Satan, with all power, signs, and lying wonders, and with all unrighteous deception among those who perish, because they did not receive the love of the truth, that they might be saved.*
> *"And for this reason God will send them strong delusion, that they should believe the lie, that they all may be condemned who did not believe the truth but had pleasure in unrighteousness."*

The Black Lives Matter ideology is dangerous. Their platform shreds the Bible—God's moral law—and replaces it with the #BLM tribal standard. Sadly, many well-meaning organizations, Christians, and churches have bought into the Black Lives Matter agenda without considering their real motive or platform.

The Bible predicted these events thousands of years ago. Those who know Biblical prophecy recognize what is happening now are the things Jesus and the Apostle Paul predicted.

The original website has been scrubbed, but I copied the quotes below before they took it down.

———

> *We are guided by the fact that all Black lives matter, regardless of actual or perceived sexual identity, gender identity, gender expression, economic status, ability, disability, religious beliefs or disbeliefs, immigration status, or location.*
> *We make space for transgender brothers and sisters to participate and lead.*
> *We are self-reflexive and do the work required to dismantle cisgender privi-*

lege and uplift Black trans folk, especially Black trans women who continue to be disproportionately impacted by trans-antagonistic violence. We build a space that affirms Black women and is free from sexism, misogyny, and environments in which men are centered.

...we dismantle the patriarchal practice that requires mothers to work "double shifts" so that they can mother in private even as they participate in public justice work.

We disrupt the Western-prescribed nuclear family structure requirement by supporting each other as extended families...

We foster a queer-affirming network. When we gather, we do so with the intention of freeing ourselves from the tight grip of heteronormative thinking, or rather, the belief that all in the world are heterosexual (unless s/he or they disclose otherwise)[i]

———

In contradiction to Biblical teachings, the last statement is disturbing: "We foster a queer-affirming network." Nowhere in the Bible does God promote a "queer" lifestyle.

The definition of "queer" in Merriam-Webster is:

1. a: Worthless, counterfeit - queer money; b: Questionable, suspicious.
2. a: Differing in some odd way from what is usual or normal; b: (1): eccentric, unconventional (2): mildly insane; c: absorbed or interested to an extreme or unreasonable degree; d: Often disparaging + offensive. (1): SEXUALLY ATTRACTED TO MEMBERS OF THE SAME SEX
3. Not quite well.

As I wrote above, I remember my first day of class in fifth grade when three black students were seated in an all-white classroom. I became good friends with one of the girls. She was a B+ student and a kind person.

However, at that time, my parents were uncomfortable with me bringing her home. My mother's comment was, "What would the neighbors say?"

That was almost sixty years ago. Most people today, including my mother, would think nothing of it. Things have changed despite the fact some want to stir up hatred and prejudice.

If you embrace the Black Lives Matter platform, I ask the reader what God will say to you. If you kneel for George Floyd or anyone but Jesus Christ, what are you saying about your faith in God?

My mother has long since admitted her response was racist, and she is no longer like that. Most people aren't. Just because a few rotten apples are racist should not taint the rest of us who are white, hard-working American patriots. I don't know anyone who has the predisposition to dislike anyone who isn't white.

However, we still need to talk about our differences without throwing each other under the bus.

One afternoon at a writer's conference, I went over to sit across the table from an African-American author who I respected. I told her I wanted to discuss racial relations and get her thoughts. When I told her I didn't see color, she said it was a racist comment—that I should see black because black is beautiful.

Her response was not what I expected. I have two daughters from another continent who look nothing like me and are not Caucasian. I don't see skin color. I don't see physical differences. I see my daughters. Why should I consciously ID everyone I meet on the basis of skin color?

I'm afraid I have to disagree with my author friend's observation, but I respect what she said. I'm learning and listening. That's the first step toward reconciliation.

In the twenty-plus years since I adopted my daughters, I've never heard a racist comment about my family. People have asked if we go together. But considering my daughters were born in Asia, and I'm about as white as they come, it's a legitimate question.

Perhaps my author friend was right; I should see black. However, everyone blends in when you live in a diverse community (my community is more varied than hers as she lives in another city).

The first thing I notice when I look at someone is not their skin color. I wonder if they are a Christian. I see them as someone I might like to know better or as my sister or brother in Christ.

I don't believe the Black Lives Matter Movement is based on racial reconciliation as they want us to believe. Demonic forces in high places are at work, stirring up the #BLM Movement (and Antifa) to cause strife, unrest, and hate.

Remember, the world today is governed by the Powers of Darkness (Satan is the power of the prince of the air), and the fallen angels empower the sons of disobedience (nonbelievers) to wage war against the sons of God (believers). Those battles can take many forms.

Tearing down statues of iconic figures from the past—people like Winston Churchill of England, Mahatma Gandhi of India, George Washington, Thomas Jefferson, and other American heroes—does nothing to help the more significant cause of promoting reconciliation and racial equality.

Were these men perfect? No. But there was one man who was—Jesus Christ, and some now want to tear down statues depicting the only perfect human being who ever lived.

Jesus Christ is the way, the truth, and the life. There is a song I love to sing with the title *They Will Know We Are Christians by Our Love.* How does that translate into action? What can we do as Christians to combat racism and prejudice?

As a starter, don't support Black Lives Matter. Their platform is divisive and goes beyond promoting racial equality to the point it discriminates against heterosexuals and the traditional American family. And that's just for starters.

I also want to point out one other important thing. Nowhere in the #BLM platform is there any mention of abortion. The fact is they do nothing to condemn it. Like Stacey Abrams from Georgia, who served in the House of Representatives from 2007 to 2017, many African American leaders are pro-choice advocates and promote the #BLM agenda, including abortion. The Planned Parenthood Oregon website touts its commitment to Black Lives Matter in the article "Our Commitment to Black Lives Matter." [ii]

If they cared about black lives, shouldn't they care about black babies? Do the lives of black babies not matter? The hypocrisy is sickening. How can #BLM advocates march (even peacefully) when they condone the killing of their black children?

According to the Arizona Capitol Times, in the article "Abortion: The Overlooked Tragedy for Black Americans," the leading cause of death in the African-American population is abortion. Don't "Baby Black Lives" matter also? If so, then why do they promote abortion? The article states: "At a ratio of 474 abortions per 1,000 live births, black women have the highest ratio of any group in the country." [iii]

We will never have good racial relations if African Americans play the "race" card and continue to see themselves as victims. If they are victims, often, it's because of their poor choices. If they remain victims, I have to ask why.

In America, out of all places, citizens have the freedom of upward mobility. That's what makes America great. Travel to Europe, Asia, the Middle East, and Africa—you won't find a single country where people have as much upward mobility to better themselves and their families as they do in the United States.

Most people don't realize the history of slavery. Slavery was an acceptable form of bondage that dates back thousands of years, even before the time of Christ. Of the millions of Africans sold into slavery worldwide, only 5% came to America, and they were the fortunate ones. Muslim countries relied heavily on enslaved people, castrated them, and turned them into eunuchs.

When the enslaved Black people outlived their usefulness, they killed them. The five percent that came to America married, bore children, and formed their own culture. Many left paganism to embrace the true God, Jesus Christ, and became believers. They wrote spirit-filled hymns and were allowed the freedom of worship.

Our country fought to end slavery in the Civil War. When that happened, we set the standard for everyone else to follow. Many countries did end slavery in the years and decades following. Our abolishment of slavery set a new worldwide standard. The last nation to outlaw slavery was Mauritania in 1981. (I recognize that slavery is still practiced in some regions of the world, but we need to focus on the norm and not the exceptions for this conversation.)

Again, as long as African Americans see themselves as victims, they will never achieve their full potential as a distinct race with God-given creativity and potential.

However, much progress has been made. Let's not condemn the excellent work already done because some in the United States want to create division and chaos. We've even had a black man serve two terms as President of the United States. That means there is no level of achievement that an African American cannot attain. When you think about it, considering the African American's humble beginnings in America, that's pretty remarkable.

Hundreds of black athletes in the NBA, NHL, MLB, and other high-profile sports make millions yearly. I doubt any of them would have achieved their dream without working hard. Playing the "victim" card wouldn't have earned them a spot on any team roster. Hard work, talent, and perseverance prevailed. There was a time when it didn't, but that's not true anymore. Team owners want the best athletes and will pay to get the most bang for their buck.

I can't think of any profession today where African Americans have not contributed their gifts and talents to pursue the American dream. It's there for the taking; my biggest fear is that our young people will settle for mediocrity rather than work hard to achieve their potential.

Like many others, I had a DNA test to discover my ancestral origins. I discovered I have African roots. One of my relatives on an ancestry website claims to be America's first black postal worker.

We are all interrelated. We all go back to Noah and his descendants. There is beauty in diversity, and there is unity in Jesus Christ.

One day last week, when I returned home, I saw my African-American neighbor pulling my trash bins up from the road and depositing them at my house. She didn't have to do that. It was kindness.

As I leaned out of the car window, I called her over and told her, "I don't care what happens in the world. You will always be my friend and neighbor."

I ended the conversation by saying, "God looks at the heart, and you have a good heart." I thought she might burst into tears.

When Jesus' disciples asked Him what the greatest commandment was, He replied:

"You shall love the LORD your God with all your heart, with
all your soul, with all your strength, and with all your
mind," and "your neighbor as yourself" (Luke 10:27).

Who is your neighbor? It's anyone in need. Just open your heart, and God will show you.

PRAYER: Abba Father, please help us to perform Good Works for the King-
dom. In doing so, may we become more like Jesus and a witness to those who are
lost and perishing.

[i] "What We Believe," Black Lives Matter," https://blacklivesmatter.com/what-we-believe/ (site removed)

[ii] "Our Commitment to Black Lives Matter," Planned Parenthood Advocates of Oregon, June 1, 2020, https://www.ppaoregon.org/2020/06/01/our-commitment-black-lives-matter/

[iii] "Abortion: The Overlooked Tragedy for Black Americans," Arizona Capitol Times, February 25, 2020, https://azcapitoltimes.com/news/2020/02/25/abortion-the-overlooked-tragedy-for-black-americans/

Chapter Thirty-Five

FINDING GOOD IN THE DARKNESS

"And there is no creature hidden from His sight, but all things
are naked and open to the eyes of Him to whom we must
give account."
Hebrews 4:13

UFOs sited in Missouri, and a man attaches dynamite to a dog and blows him up. (He survived and is being taken care of by a Good Samaritan who renamed him Rocket). A man bites off parts of another man's face, and the UN calls for an emergency meeting to deal with the crisis in Syria.

These are just some of the news items of the day. If I were an alien in a UFO passing by, I would hightail it and find another planet for vacationing.

On a more serious note, how can we listen to the news stories that bombard us daily and not become despondent?

Many years ago, at a Christian writer's conference, an editor asked me what I did for a living.

I said to him, "I provide closed captioning for television."

His eyes lit up. "There must be plenty of writing material in those juicy stories."

I laughed. "What good stories can I write? Frequently, the news leaves me depressed."

And if you are anything like me, I'm sure you feel the same.

Nathanael expressed a similar sentiment when he commented about Jesus' birthplace,

"Can anything good come out of Nazareth" (John 1:46)?

But my response to that editor has always bothered me.

Can I not find good in the world if I look for it? Does God not bring good out of evil? Can He not redeem the worst story I've ever captioned?

Sometimes, when falling asleep at night, I will think back to something I captioned during the day and be troubled. Perhaps it's Satan's way of attacking me; if he can make me doubt God's sufficiency, how effective can I be in my witness?

In my human understanding, I feel or see the pain and suffering inflicted. And while I despise someone else's gross behavior, what about when I hurt others? Sometimes, I wonder how God puts up with us. How can He not get angry? If I have a righteous indignation in my human wisdom, how much more so does God?

That brings me to a recent news story out of Canada. I do not want to mention the man's name because I don't want to give him any notoriety. This criminal allegedly murdered a student from China, cut up his body, and shipped his body parts to various schools and government offices in Canada. He then flew to France and later Germany, where an astute Internet cafe employee in Berlin spotted him and contacted the local police. He is now sitting in jail awaiting extradition back to Canada.

While the case is tragic, can I find good in this horrific story?

What are the chances that this fugitive who fled from Canada would be spotted and recognized by another individual across the Atlantic?

This story prompted me to ask, how much news gets shared on the Internet, television, and radio? How many people board planes each day?

According to several sources, if you are curious, there are 175 million active users on Twitter. 1,966,514,816 people use the Internet, 12 million people watch television daily, 261 million Americans listen to the radio, and over three million board planes.

These figures are mind-boggling, and when you consider there are eight billion people in the world, you wonder how one person could be significant. Who am I that God should take notice of me in my little corner of Northeast Florida? And yet, God doesn't need a phone, TV, Internet, or any other device to find anyone.

Each of us does matter to God. How many more people could this murderer (if found guilty of his alleged crime) have hurt were it not for this Internet cafe employee in Berlin? I'm sure this man did not wake up that morning and say to a friend, "I'm going to turn in one of the world's most sought-after criminals today."

In I Corinthians 2:7-8, the Bible speaks of God having secret wisdom:

> *"But we speak the wisdom of God in a mystery, the hidden* wisdom *which God ordained before the ages for our glory, which none of the rulers of this age knew; for had they known, they would not have crucified the Lord of glory."*

Paul seems to be saying it was necessary for the religious leaders who crucified Jesus not to understand the gravity of their deeds. Jesus needed to die for our sins. Perhaps that's a hint for us today when we cry to God that we don't understand. Maybe God's ultimate plan is hidden. The burden of knowledge is too significant. Only Jesus could bear our cross that He willingly took upon Himself so we would not be condemned.

In Matthew 24:12, when referring to the latter days and the signs of the end of the age, Jesus stated:

> *"And because lawlessness will abound, the love of many will grow cold."*

We might think, "Oh, I will always love my neighbor, family, and husband."

But we see the darkness increasing all around us; we hear horror stories every night, like the burning of Lahaina on the Island of Maui. We don't understand how something like this could happen. We know those days are coming that Jesus talked about.

Simon Peter said in John 6:68:

"Lord, to whom shall we go? You have the words of eternal life."

Our faith must be strong enough to stand up to the worst of humanity because Satan is relentless. God has already sealed his fate, and he has nothing to lose. Whenever I start to doubt, I remind myself the Kingdom of God is within me (Luke 17:21), and the battle belongs to the Lord (II Chronicles 20:15).

God told us what the world would be like before His return through His prophets, so we shouldn't be dismayed or discouraged. I take comfort knowing the world is not out of God's control, and criminals can't escape His watchful eye.

I'm sure it was not by luck that God used a Good Samaritan to catch this fugitive. May we be comforted knowing that nothing escapes an all-knowing God who is everywhere all the time.

PRAYER: Abba Father, may we be Your faithful watchmen and women on the wall, performing Good Works even in the darkness.

Chapter Thirty-Six

DOCTORS, "SMART PEOPLE" AND COVID-19

*"For nation will rise against nation, and kingdom against king-
dom. And there will be famines, pestilences, and earthquakes
in various places."*
Matthew 24:7

A good author friend in Melbourne, Australia, asked, "Why are doctors
not hearing from God like you and me? People here [in Australia] are
giving up their freedoms and receiving the jab without question."

His question is one that few at that time asked. The most severely
locked-down state in the world, Victoria, Australia, was reminiscent of
Nazi Germany. Anyone who didn't receive the jab couldn't participate
in everyday life.

My friend said the Australians took the jab without question,
without thought, and without concern about the totalitarian nature of
enforcement, even for those who didn't want it.

Maybe God is speaking to those people, but they aren't listening.

When you read through the Old Testament—Jeremiah and Ezekiel,
for example—the people did not listen to the prophets. Despite all the
warnings, the people didn't heed the dire predictions from God and
chose to go their own way.

If you remember the movie *The Matrix*, those who swallowed the red pill knew the truth. Those who took the blue pill lived in a virtual reality without an awareness of the evil Matrix. If *The Matrix's* victims had known their reality wasn't real, would they have chosen to continue in the Matrix, or would they have chosen to live in truth no matter how difficult or painful?

These types of movies are often predictive of future events. I wonder if God gives us a foreshadowing through various media about future times to warn us, in much the same way the Old Testament prophets exhorted the wayward Israelites.

Of course, we know Hollywood is full of occultists, and while Satan is not omniscient, he knows enough to infiltrate people's thoughts to believe he's as wise as God.

Fast forward to today. Many people have turned off the news. Some have awakened to realize much of what they are told isn't true. Despite knowing they have been lied to, many still prefer to live in ignorance. Never mind the truth, morality, or the ultimate purpose of the globalists or whoever is in power.

We must remember Satan only knows what God allows him to know, and God has given the "prince of the power of the air" the ability to deceive those who can be beguiled. He must have worked overtime from January 2020 till September 2023 as I'm writing this.

I have often said God is gracious because He doesn't give us all the truth in one fell swoop. If we were all-knowing, that knowledge would destroy us. Remember Adam and Eve's sin in the garden, wanting to be like God? Our moral compass rooted in the Scriptures can fail us when encountering evil.

Said in another way, the fallen nature of man is so vile that complete knowledge of evil would destroy us. I see an animal get abused, and it devastates me. To witness a child suffer or be a pawn for an ignoble purpose is unconscionable. To even think about abortion makes me sick to my stomach.

I remember what Jesus said about those who hurt a child:

> "But whoever causes one of these little ones who believe in Me to
> stumble, it would be better for him if a millstone were hung

around his neck, and he were thrown into the sea" (Mark 9:42).

To address COVID-19 specifically, the push for a mandatory vaccine was NOT about a vaccine. The mRNA is NOT a vaccine. It's a tool. It's laying the foundation for implementing the Mark of the Beast in the future Tribulation. This whole system must be in place BEFORE the anti-Christ makes his appearance.

I will add a little levity to this dire topic. When I went through breast cancer treatment, I had a double mastectomy. I opted to have a plastic surgeon do reconstruction with the surgery.

Anyone who has had a surgical procedure knows the physician visits the patient on the morning of the surgery to talk to the patient about what will happen. My plastic surgeon came in per the usual protocol, and I asked him how long his part of the procedure would take.

He said, "A couple of hours."

I was surprised. "That long?"

He replied, "Well, we can't just shove it up there."

There are many dots to connect and threads to thread and technological innovations (that need patents) that must be in place to facilitate the work of the anti-Christ and his partner in crime. The evil one can't just "shove things into place." Satan has been working on this project ever since the Garden of Eden, but we are close to the culmination of this epic battle between Good and evil.

Most Christians don't know this stuff because they DON'T WANT to know. Almost one-third of the Bible is prophetic, and yet, how many Christians have read the Book of Revelation or studied the Old Testament prophets?

It doesn't take a rocket scientist to figure out that things are not as they appear. Or perhaps it's the biased nature of the media, highly skilled at editorializing facts, that spins the news to fit their version of the truth. However, any thinking individual can see right through the deception—if they want to.

Historical documents reveal how Hitler used the media to push his Nazi agenda and indoctrinate the youth. His propaganda was imbued in the educational system, and his youth camps tapped into idyllic dreams of nirvana. Germans longed to see a renewed vision of their country's future after Germany's humiliating defeat in World War I.

I said years ago the media would be part of the beast system. If you agree with their agenda, the media gives you a platform to speak, and they put a mic in front of your mouth.

> *"And he was given a mouth speaking great things and blasphemies, and he was given authority to continue for forty-two months" (Revelation 13:5).*

When it came to the COVID-19 vaccine, the pharmaceutical companies, the CDC, the FDA, the NIH, and the WHO were in cahoots with one of the wealthiest men in the world, Bill Gates. Many people don't realize drug companies have no liability if a vaccine injures a person. Liability ensures accountability. We don't have that anymore (we once did), even though big pharma has made millions from vaccines.

The pharmaceutical giants pay millions to the news media to advertise their drugs. What commercials do you see on TV all the time? The networks push big pharma because those commercials pay their salaries.

I don't believe the unbiased mainstream media will ever come back because THEY DON'T WANT to come back. Why should they? Is there an economic incentive to tell people the truth? Do the media conglomerates have enough moral chutzpah to question the pharmaceutical companies' data who pay their bills and keep them on the air?

It was not just the news media held hostage. The unfortunate victims trickled all the way down to your physician. Many doctors were subjected to fines and revocation of their licenses if they prescribed Ivermectin or didn't follow the guidelines of the CDC. Some faced threats to themselves and their family. At the very least, they received verbal reprimands that often escalated to the licensing boards. Most doctors chose to accept the status quo.

Besides that, how many doctors want to take on the medical establishment? Perhaps they are too comfortable living in virtual reality.

They make big money, live in expensive houses, and have kids to educate.

So they went along with the narrative, and after a while, they believed it. Physicians and nurses had to believe it because how would they live with themselves if they didn't? What about that Hippocratic Oath?

What about the thousands of doctors who denied Ivermectin to hospitalized patients who might have lived if they had received early treatment? What about the man in my church who died from COVID-19? The hospital refused to offer him Ivermectin despite his wife's pleas.

Again, why would they deny possible life-saving treatment? The NIH could not issue an Emergency Use Authorization for a new vaccine if other treatments were available. The EUA enabled pharmaceutical companies to skip some of the vaccine protocols that had been followed for decades.

That's why they shut down Trump when he started talking about hydrochlorothiazide. A year later, the narrative continued across America. Hospitals were not allowed to give Ivermectin to patients for COVID-19 because they said it was an off-label use and prohibited.

In reality, doctors use drugs in off-label ways all the time. But if hospitals or doctors prescribed it for COVID-19, they were in trouble.

For a loved one to receive Ivermectin in the hospital, the only option was for the family to go to court and get a court order, and even then, the road was treacherous. Hospitals continued to put up roadblocks. Why?

If Ivermectin worked (like so many doctors worldwide have documented), how could the medical community in America justify the thousands of patients they denied it to? That would be akin to saying they allowed them to die. Do your own research on this topic, preferably with a different search engine than Google. Be prepared to swallow the red pill. You won't like what you see.

I replied to my Australian friend, who asked, "Why are doctors not hearing from God like you and me?" My answer still is, "Because they don't want to." They have justified the means, making people take the jab, to achieve their (hospital, drug companies, et cetera) goal of making money. It runs roughshod over our individual freedoms, particularly here in America. A few people fought back and paid dearly.

Governments rarely give power back to their people once they seize it. Will my daughters know the freedoms I've enjoyed for a lifetime? I don't know, but as my mother says, "They won't know any different."

My way of fighting back is to stay in the Word, pray unceasingly, encourage friends, and witness when I can. I acknowledge that most of what I hear and see through the media isn't true. And I know things will continue down this slippery slope until the Tribulation. We may slow things down if we pray and ask God for mercy.

But I must ask, do I want to? I'm ready for Jesus to return now. I can't wait for Him to execute justice in this fallen world. I can't wait to see my Savior, who died on the cross for me (and you) over two thousand years ago.

I don't know if we can delay what's coming. But I know God wants us to be busy witnessing and bringing souls into the Kingdom of God. There isn't anything more important than where we will spend eternity.

Returning to the conversation with my Australian friend, why do I see the truth and others don't?

If you look at the gifts of the Spirit, one relates to knowledge.

"For to one is given the word of wisdom through the Spirit, to another the word of knowledge through the same spirit" (I Corinthians 12:8).

I am not a prophet and would never want to be, but I do believe God, on a few occasions, has given me a "Word of Knowledge" about things or insights that were beyond my natural ability to perceive.

I also think, and this is just me speaking, creative people have a sensate spirit. In other words, they "feel" things the average person doesn't perceive. They feel it in their soul.

History is replete with examples. People write books, paint paintings, and sing songs that capture the essence of reality long before the typical person trying to "survive" is even aware of what's happening.

Perhaps the creativity of these gifted people is even part of the movement, inching society forward because that's how change happens. An emotional catharsis arises. Sometimes, it leads to war; other times, it leads to social revolution.

We are experiencing that now. Christian authors who have been writing for the glory of God can't help but be aware of the increasing evilness everywhere. God mysteriously gives us insights we can use to glorify Him that others would probably squander who are happy to swallow the blue pill (*The Matrix*).

I've probably put the reader to sleep with my ramblings, but my Australian friend asked a great question: Why do some people see what's happening and others don't? There isn't a simple answer—yet. But we need to keep asking the question.

Might I end with the most important question—where will you, the reader, spend eternity? This world is passing away, but the glory of the Lord is forever.

Don't leave Earth without accepting Jesus Christ into your heart. He longs to have a personal relationship with you. Give your life to Him, turn from your sin, and don't look back. The Lord's return is very, very soon. Today is the day of salvation.

PRAYER: Dear Jesus, please help us to discern the times. Help us to keep our eyes on You. We will live with discouragement if we don't look up. Help us to live each day for You and reflect Your love to those who are perishing.

Chapter Thirty-Seven

BRAVE NEW WORLD OF COVID-19 AND THE COMING MARK OF THE BEAST

"For to be carnally minded is death, but to be spiritually minded is life and peace."
Romans 8:6

———

"If the earth-dwellers receive the Mark of the Beast, they can't be saved. I believe it changes human DNA, and you are no longer imagers of God. You are a Chimera." *-Lorilyn Roberts*

———

Why would I make such a bold statement? First, receiving the Mark of the Beast means you have decided to worship the Beast and not Jesus Christ.

A chimera is someone or something that has received a transfer of genetically and immunologically different tissue, i.e., joining two species into one.

If a person receives the Mark of the Beast and changes his mind, he can't undo it. He will spend eternity in hell. A person's heart may be so hardened he's beyond redemption, but we must also remember that Jesus died for humans, not chimera, Nephilim, angels, hybrids, or humanoids.

I believe the Mark of the Beast corrupts human DNA—so much that a human being is no longer human. When he worships the Beast, perhaps not only a physical change happens but also a spiritual decadence that is irreversible.

God is a God of mercy, and the Scriptures tell us if a person is repentant and accepts Jesus Christ into his heart, he is born again. How many has Jesus saved out of the occult? How many have come to believe in Jesus, who worshipped Allah, Buddha, or Shiva?

Something must be significantly different about the Mark of the Beast and worshipping the Antichrist. Is it a tattoo or something physical? Is it something genetic, or is it something only spiritual?

> "He [the second Beast] was granted the power to give breath to the image of the [first] Beast, that the image of the Beast should both speak and cause as many as would not worship the image of the Beast to be killed. He causes all, both small and great, rich and poor, free and slave, to receive a mark on their right hand or their foreheads, and that no one may buy or sell except one who has the mark or the name of the Beast, or the number of his name. Here is wisdom. Let him who has understanding calculate the number of the Beast, for it is the number of man: His number is 666"
> Revelation 13:15-18.

> "And the smoke of their torment ascends forever and ever; and they have no rest day or night, who worship the beast and his image, and whoever receives the mark of his name"
> Revelation 14:11.

These Scriptures emphasize anyone who receives the Mark of the Beast can't be saved. I believe God will remove all Born-Again Christians before this happens. Of course, there is disagreement about the rapture's timing, but my thoughts align with Jan Markell, Amir Tsarfati, JD Farag, Jack Hibbs, Brandon Holthaus, and many other evangelical Christians. We won't be here.

I want to explain my view on this further. It is evident from Scripture the Beast does not seize absolute control until the second half of the Tribulation. That means the first three and a half years of the seven-year Tribulation have passed before the Antichrist demands worship through His Mark and the Beast system.

The timing of the Abomination of Desolation, when the Antichrist goes into the temple and desecrates it, strongly indicates that he has withdrawn his covenant with the Jews and now claims he is the only one to be worshipped. The Beast system would need to be in place for this event to transpire.

> "Therefore when you see the 'abomination of desolation,' spoken of by Daniel the prophet, standing in the holy place (whoever reads, let him understand), then let those who are in Judea flee to the mountains. Let him who is on the housetop not go down to take anything out of his house. And let him who is in the field not go back to get his clothes.
> "But woe to those who are pregnant and to those who are nursing babies in those days! And pray that your flight may not be in winter or on the Sabbath.
> "For then there will be **great Tribulation** [emphasis mine], such as has not been since the beginning of the world until this time, no, nor ever shall be.
> "And unless those days were shortened, no flesh would be saved; but for the elect's sake those days will be shortened" (Matthew 24:15-22).

According to this passage, the Great Tribulation starts in the middle of the seven years (when the 'abomination of desolation' happens), and it covers the last half of the Tribulation. At this point, the Antichrist reveals his true agenda and identity when he desecrates the Jewish temple and demands worship.

The Mark of the Beast will be how he controls the world's nations. As I write this today, in 2023, I believe the Mark of the Beast is years away. The Tribulation has not begun and won't until the Antichrist makes a covenant with Israel (Daniel 9:27).

If you study the timeline of the seven-year Tribulation, you will also see the final (bowl) judgments commence at about the same time—the midway point of the Tribulation.

Some have questioned whether the COVID-19 vaccine might be the Mark of the Beast. While the COVID-19 vaccine differs from all other vaccines, I do not believe it is. The relevant question is: Can it change human DNA?

The COVID-19 vaccine has introduced "concerning" new technologies. Bill Gates and Microsoft applied for a new patent on June 20, 2019, and it was granted international status on April 22, 2020. The patent number is 060606. Below is a link to an article that discusses the patent application. However, the Bill and Melinda Gates Foundation lifted the patent protections on coronavirus technologies under mounting pressure and scrubbed much information related to the patent application.

https://orientalreview.org/2020/04/29/bill-gates-vaccinations-microchips-and-patent-060606/ (No longer a working link).

Because this is a controversial topic, I've included a second link that presents the same information from another source on Facebook. It's marked as "not accurate," but that's due to the heightened censoring we see across the media. As of this writing, the link is still available.[1]

Notice in the dead link the word "microchips." Even if the patent does not include the insertion of a microchip into the human body, which I was not able to confirm or deny, the patent, in lay language, does allow for the user to receive money (cryptocurrency) in exchange for allowing access to a person's body biometrics via an app that can monitor a person's activity (more information on this later).

The patent, "Cryptocurrency System Using Body Activity Data," was registered on March 26, 2020. I spent a lot of time trying to understand its significance. Here is my interpretation of where this is going, and you can decide if this technology could be used to implement the Mark of the Beast.

Based on my research (I am a Berean, not a scientist), I don't believe the Moderna and Pfizer vaccines use quantum dots. However, if they aren't now, that's the goal. Specifically, the Bill and Melinda Gates Foundation wants to use an "implantable quantum dot microneedle vaccination delivery system" to emit a unique kind of invisible UV light called Luciferase. An enzyme produces the light and is necessary for the mobile app to work.

To encourage people to be vaccinated or engage in other necessary activities, Big Brother can reward the person for his excellent behavior using cryptocurrency, which is part of the 060606 patent.

Before cryptocurrency can be introduced globally, a digital currency must follow an economic collapse. If control were from a centralized location, the power would be worldwide—just as the Bible predicts.

If you were China (atheistic government) or Germany (Nazi history), Russia (Communist government), Italy (Fascist history), or Japan (Imperial history), you would want to wield this power. You would do whatever it took to enforce your mandates by making people powerless. You would hide your ultimate agenda through censoring. In a country like America, the only country with a Bill of Rights, you would have "test runs" to see how much freedom people would forego to have peace and security.

It's all about control. The World Economic Forum held a conference planning and executing war games about a worldwide pandemic in October 2019—right before COVID-19 hit the world stage.

The COVID-19 pandemic was a globalist pandemic. In a sense, the world became more united than at any other time in human history,

I don't believe the COVID-19 vaccine accomplished the purpose for which the globalists manufactured and patented it. In my sanctified imagination, the only way to move forward with their agenda is to have another worldwide pandemic with a mandatory vaccine. During the COVID-19 lockdown, 105 of 193 countries pushed for compulsory vaccines. Perhaps next time, all 193 countries will abide by the mandated rules of those dressed in white.

The elitists did everything they could to maximize their control. Fear played a considerable role. People wore masks like their lives depended on them. I believe a similar protocol is in place that will be followed in the future.

The next step in this evolving process was keeping up with those exposed to COVID-19. The government set up contact tracing to do this. Suppose you could make contact tracing electronic? You could monitor every person on the Earth for COVID-19. If you could do it for COVID-19, you could do it for anything.

If you look at what the Bible says about the Mark of the Beast, the technology is being perfected now and will be in place when the Antichrist becomes the world leader, as foretold in Scripture.

The COVID-19 vaccine and "plandemic of 2020" is just the beginning—a pseudo-pandemic to set the stage for something more sinister. The end goal is world control, but people must be conditioned and seduced into believing the government is their savior.

The ultimate goal of the globalists is to turn people into sheeple—useful idiots who believe the lies the media tells them. The masses will be deceived as a result of rejecting God. They will prefer to seek their identity in tribal affiliation, the occult, or sexual perversion. Of course, people inclined that way will speak in neutral terms, more classically referenced as double-speak in George Orwell's *1984*.

The Bible has much to say about what the world will be like in the last days. Here are a couple of quotes.

> *"because, although they knew God, they did not glorify* Him *as God, nor were thankful, but became futile in their thoughts, and their foolish hearts were darkened.*
> *"Professing to be wise, they became fools, and changed the glory of the incorruptible God into an image made like corruptible man—and birds and four-footed animals and creeping things" (Romans 1:21-23).*

Noah and his immediate family were the only ones in that day whose bloodlines were not contaminated. Jesus said in Matthew 24:37:

> *"But as the days of Noah were, so also will the coming of the Son of Man be."*

So that begs the question, does the COVID-19 vaccine have the potential to change DNA?

If the COVID-19 vaccine doesn't, something on the horizon will. However, let me add this one thought. Bill Gates' patent for the "Implantable Quantum Dot Microneedle Vaccination Delivery System" uses a light-bearing enzyme called Luciferase.

Technically, it's a semiconductor. A semiconductor is used in electronics. Their conductivity value lies between copper and glass. Central Processing Units, more commonly known as CPUs, are used as semiconductors in computers. You can see where I am going with this.

Even if the Pfizer and Moderna vaccines are not currently using quantum dot technology, it doesn't take much for any thinking individual to connect the dots (pun intended). That's where all of this is going.

Again, I want to emphasize the COVID-19 vaccine is NOT the Mark of the Beast, but it is preparing the way. Because the Bible passages referenced above mention worshiping the "image" of the Beast, there must be a connection between the brain, a computerized image, and a "mark" intertwined with our DNA.

> "Then I heard a loud voice from the temple saying to the seven angels, 'Go and pour out the bowls of the wrath of God on the earth.' So the first went and poured out his bowl [first bowl judgment] upon the earth, and a foul and loathsome sore came upon the men who had the mark of the Beast and those who worshiped his image" (Revelation 16:1-2).

Could the "loathsome sore" be a vaccine injury? When I received the smallpox vaccine, the vaccine mark stayed on my skin for years. Tattoos used to be taboo but have become prevalent in modern society. Almost every young person has one. Leviticus 19:28 says:

> "You shall not make any cuttings in your flesh for the dead, nor tattoo any marks on you: I am the LORD."

While I'm not judging tattooing, it has a historical precedent associated with evil. One only needs to look back at World War II and the Nazi practice of tattooing the Jews. The purpose of the ID was to identify and track them. History repeats itself. I would not be surprised to see a digital version of this practice connected with Bill Gates' 060606 patent.

In China, everyone has a social score. Your score is based on how you live your life according to the government's demands. You can access better jobs, schools, and education with a higher social score.

Suppose the government could track your every move and monitor your daily body activity via a vaccination delivery system that is readable on a mobile app? In that case, I can see America adopting a similar social score system. There is already talk about it. Big Brother only needs a reason—like it used Covid-19 to implement contact tracing.

Again, this new mRNA vaccine technology is the gateway to a more ominous future technology. While the CDC and other sites state the COVID-19 vaccine does not change human DNA, I'm skeptical. I know the CDC has not been forthright about traditional vaccines. Don't believe me? Watch the movie *VAXXED*.

I purchased a viewing of *VAXXED* on YouTube a couple of years ago and was going to link it here, but I can no longer find it. Doesn't it make you wonder why YouTube and other social media sites want to censor this information? Could it be the government doesn't want you to know the truth?

My younger daughter had a seizure after receiving the MMR vaccine. We spent several hours in the emergency room when she underwent a CT scan. Thankfully, it was negative, but when I told the doctor I thought it was related to the five vaccines she received in one doctor's visit a week earlier, he told me she would have to be one in a hundred thousand. I looked at him and said, "Then she's one in a hundred thousand."

She should never have received five vaccines at once (despite my concerns, the nurse assured me it was safe), and the literature on adverse reactions to vaccines has been suppressed. If you want to learn more, you can watch this excellent debate between Robert Kennedy Jr. and Allen Dershowitz, discussing both sides of the vaccine argument.[2]

I know I've covered a lot of information, but perhaps this is a wake-up call for people to do their own research. To finish, I want to point out a few more observations that struck me as significant when the Mark of the Beast spoken of in the Book of Revelation is made mandatory.

First, the Beast (Antichrist) has total power when he makes the Mark compulsory and worship of him is absolute. Isn't that what the globalist agenda is about, a one-world government with complete control and allegiance?

Second, the image of the Beast relates to technology. The two Beasts (the Antichrist and the false prophet) control all the technology. Think drones, 5-G, the worldwide web (666 in Hebrew numerology), iPhones, computers, and even medicine. Corona means crown in Latin.

Remember the four horsemen of the apocalypse? The first horse was white, and the rider wore a crown. Who wears a white coat and fights battles of life and death? Is there any correlation? Sometimes, Scripture has more than one meaning.

Third, no one can buy or sell without the Mark. That means the two beasts control the entire economy on the planet. Could this be via a form of cryptocurrency? How convenient Bill Gates' patent would be to reward people for their excellent behavior via cryptocurrency.

Fourth, some don't bow to the Beast or worship him but keep the commandments of God. That it requires "patient endurance" speaks to unimaginable persecution and suffering that extends for a period of time.(Revelation 14:12).

Fifth, there will be rich people and poor people, enslaved people and free people, great people and lowly people who receive the Mark (Revelation 13:16). This makes me believe capitalism will still exist. A communist takeover of all countries won't happen before the ascension of the Antichrist. That gives me hope as we see the erosion of our freedoms in America and around the world.

> *"And Jesus answered and said to them: 'Take heed that no one deceives you'"* *(Matthew 24:4).*

Implying in the last days, many will be deceived. A brave new world is upon us. As Jesus said, we must be "wise as serpents and harmless as doves" (Matthew 10:16).

How that plays out, I'm not sure. I imagine it will be different for each one of us. Whatever that is, knowledge is power, and God told Daniel in the last days "knowledge will increase" (Daniel 12:4).

God has given us the ability to know His wisdom. Keep looking up; Jesus is coming soon.

PRAYER: Dear Jesus, will we remain faithful when we see what's coming? The Bible says the spirit is willing, but the body is weak. May we not live in fear but in love, for perfect love casts out fear. Help us to spread the Gospel while we still have time. And if You tarry, please help us to persevere and cling to Your Good Word, knowing it is trustworthy and true.

Chapter Thirty-Eight

HITLER AND COVID-19 - THE PARALLELS ARE STARTLING

"For I will gather all the nations to battle against Jerusalem;
The city shall be taken, The houses rifled, And the women
ravished.
"Half of the city shall go into captivity, But the remnant of the
people shall not be cut off from the city."
(Zechariah 14:2)

When I was in high school and learned about the Holocaust, I asked two questions, even at my young age: How could someone as evil as Hitler rise to power and do what he did, and how could the masses let him do it?

When COVID-19 was past its peak, I visited my family in Atlanta. My sister's husband was airing *The Complete Story of Hitler and the Nazis*. I was drawn into the docudrama and couldn't believe the parallels between Germany and what happened in America from the onslaught of COVID-19.

Some of the parallels include the following:

———

1. How quickly Germany changed once Hitler came to power.
    PARALLEL: Overnight, America changed with COVID-19.

2. Hitler wanted to make the German race pure Aryan by eliminating the Jews. Less well-known is he also murdered the old, infirmed, frail, sick, and those who were physically, mentally, and emotionally challenged.
    PARALLEL: Doctors and hospitals followed directives from Dr. Anthony Fauci to give Remdesivir to COVID-19 patients, which, in effect, had a higher mortality rate than other less expensive, life-saving drugs like hydrochlorothiazide and Ivermectin. Of all the drugs Dr. Anthony Fauci could have chosen, he chose the least effective drug for treating COVID-19.[1]

3. Hitler possessed a hypnotic power over the nation. Trusting people were deceived by his charisma, authoritative persona, and sweeping agenda.
    PARALLEL: In America, everything Dr. Anthony Fauci, the CDC, the FDA, and the NIH recommended were followed without question, without discussion, and without exception.

    Not just laypeople (who may have had justification if their only source of information was the biased media), but doctors, nurses, pharmacists, hospitals, and almost every medical establishment in America. Whatever Dr. Anthony Fauci said was what everyone believed to be accurate. Few people spoke out against COVID-19 medical tyranny; if they did, they were censored and annihilated in one form or another.

4. Hitler took away the rights of the German people.
    PARALLEL: During COVID-19, governments worldwide seized control over citizens and forced them to live subhuman lives—wearing masks, limiting their travel, forced isolation, and, in some instances, tracking those exposed to COVID-19.

. . .

5. Hitler shut down churches and dismantled Christian institutions, encouraging the worship of him and his Nazi party. "Heil Hitler!" was a form of worship and idolatry.

PARALLEL: During COVID-19, worldwide, churches were shuttered. Some still have not reopened.

6. Hitler abolished freedom of speech.

PARALLEL: Today, if you criticize the US government, whether national or state, even down to local school board meetings, you're branded a domestic terrorist. Who could have imagined that a non-elected medical complex would pave the way for the censorship we've endured since COVID-19?

7. Millions died because of Hitler's actions.

PARALLEL: In America, almost one million people suffered or died from the COVID-19 vaccines. I wrote a piece about this with many links to multiple sources. When I posted a tweet linked to my editorial page, Twitter removed my post, saying it violated Twitter rules.

8. Hitler divided the masses between the Aryan race and the "deplorables." Does that remind you of Hillary Clinton calling Trump supporters "deplorables"?

PARALLEL: Division is the name of the game—black versus white, vaxxed versus unvaxxed, compliant versus non-compliant, red states versus blue states, Democrats versus Republicans, liberal versus conservative—and gender dysphoria. People want to be something they aren't.

9. Hitler wanted power.

PARALLEL: We have globalists in Washington and worldwide who want to take away our freedoms, including home ownership, and make us subservient to a few. Remember the World Economic Forum motto: "You will own nothing, and you will be happy."

10. Hitler's maniacal vision led to World War II, leading to the deaths of almost 80 million people.

PARALLEL: If history is cyclical, and we know it is, we will face World War III within three years based on the self-serving grandiose globalists' policies.

11. Because there was occult influence behind Hitler's rise to power, I will end on number 11 to make the point.

PARALLEL: A demonic agenda was behind the COVID-19 "plandemic." The word for "pharma" in the Bible is sorcery. The second part of Revelation 18:23 says, "For your merchants were the great men of the earth, for by your sorcery all the nations were deceived."

———

———

Jesus said in Matthew 24:4:

"Take heed that no man deceives you."

The only way not to be deceived is to be a Berean. Study God's Word, pray in the spirit, and be aware of what's happening worldwide in light of Biblical prophecy. If the German Christians had done these things, they would have had the Holy Spirit's power to revolt against Hitler and his diabolical madness.

At the very least, they might have stopped trains on the way to the death camps. Instead, the pastors would tell the congregations to sing loudly to drown out the victims' cries as they passed by.

What can you do in your corner of the world to make a difference? Ask God. And He will show you.

PRAYER: Our Father, as Your ambassador, please help us to find our purpose in You. Governments call ambassadors home before wars start, so help us quickly bring the Kingdom of God to those in darkness. Let us shout the Good News from the rooftops if that's what it takes. Please use us, Lord.

Chapter Thirty-Nine

REFLECTIONS ON COVID-19 IN SEPTEMBER 2023

*"Behold, I [Jesus Christ] send you out as sheep in the midst of
wolves. Therefore be wise as serpents and harmless as
doves."*
Matthew 10:16

The world has moved on from COVID-19, but we will feel the
ramifications for years. We want to believe the disease is behind us—
after all, who wants to relive it? But it is here permanently in one form
or another. Perhaps it will reappear under a different name, but we
know various strains of COVID-19 are here to stay.

What concerns me more is the number of people who took the
vaccine. No one can deny the uptick in heart-related deaths among
young people, but the news media is not covering it. I have a remedy
for that if you read my key points below.

I'm sure others could come up with more suggestions, but this is
my list as a starting point to hold the government, the medical profession, the pharmaceutical companies, and the media accountable.
When the next manufactured pandemic happens, we don't want to
experience the devastating effects of government control, loss of free-

doms, and brandishing of people like me who refused to take the vaccine.

———

If I were to sum up my thoughts, here are some key points.

1. The government needs to keep its nose out of the medical profession and allow doctors to practice medicine without feeling threatened, worried about losing their jobs, or written off as incompetent when they disagree with the "official narrative."

2. Big tech (including Google, Facebook, and Twitter) must stop colluding with the government and the media to control the narrative of what people are told and censoring what people say. I thought we had free speech in America.

3. Pharmaceutical companies need to be held accountable for the injuries and deaths caused by the COVID-19 vaccines, and the government should never implement an emergency use authorization again. The emergency authorization limited the pharmaceutical companies' liability, and they made billions from the vaccines. The drug companies must be transparent with the public about their protocols, what's in the vaccines, and what people groups the trial vaccines did not cover. For example, the trials did not include pregnant women, and I captioned infomercials where reporters said they were safe for pregnant women. I quit captioning news for two years after I wrote that on a broadcast. When I start writing lies, that's when I stop captioning.

4 The media shouldn't be allowed paid advertising by pharmaceutical companies.

. . .

5. The government should not quarantine healthy people. At-risk people should be.

6. An independent agency should investigate the CDC, FDA, NIH, WHO, and the government's roll-out of the COVID-19 vaccines.

7. Dr. Anthony Fauci should go to jail.

8. A qualified, unbiased, non-governmental oversight committee should examine the massive spike in heart-related deaths since the COVID-19 vaccines.

———

I could go on, but this will happen again unless we take steps to avoid repeating our mistakes: Another pandemic, more vaccines, more control; this is just the beginning.

Everyone knows when the pandemic began, older people and high-risk groups died from COVID-19. Thus, the media, the government, and the medical community pursued a vaccine, but hospitals and doctors denied treatment to patients with protocols that could have helped, like Ivermectin. Why didn't Africa have as many deaths as the rest of the world? Because they used Ivermectin to treat it.

The worst part is what the hospitals did recommend: Remdesivir. Remdesivir destroyed people's kidneys, and 50% of the patients who took the drug died or suffered significant injuries.

One of my daughters had neurocysticercosis at seven years old. The first time I went on the Internet, I searched for how to treat neurocysticercosis, downloaded the article from the University of Florida Medical School Library, and printed it. I gave it to her primary care doctor and asked if we could use that protocol.

Initially, the doctors wanted to do surgery. I said no. We sought a second opinion from a Yale infectious disease expert. The Yale doctor consulted with the doctors who wrote the article I found online, and she shared her conclusion with the doctors treating my daughter. After quite an intense couple of weeks, including taking my daughter to the Yale Infectious Disease Clinic in Connecticut, Shands followed the protocol I wanted.

My daughter, in medical parlance, was considered a "zebra." Nobody was sure what to do. The surgeons weren't going to do surgery, not on my watch. Not without a second, third, or fourth opinion. A few years earlier, doctors diagnosed my father with a brain tumor. He had surgery and died fifteen months later. I prayed my heart out for my daughter to have a different result.

I'm sharing this because the patient and the family should always have the final say in treating a patient after weighing all the alternatives presented to them by medical experts. That is not the case anymore. I no longer trust the medical profession. In fact, I hardly trust anyone. Jesus said the number one thing that would mark the last days is deception.

We live in an age of deceit. We must question everything and never assume what people tell us is the truth, especially concerning matters of life and death.

If I could make one more recommendation, it would be this: Never inject another vaccine into your body unless it's one of the very few that we know is safe and effective, like tetanus and polio. Until a healthy discourse is allowed again on controversial topics, I fear what awaits us when the next pandemic hits. It won't be pretty. Without transparency, who knows what's really in those vaccines?

PRAYER: Dear Jesus, please give us wisdom to know the truth in all things. Help us to be as harmless as doves and as wise as serpents.

Chapter Forty

TRUMP, BIDEN, MEDIA, GLOBALIZATION, ISRAEL, ABORTION, AND HITLER

"'When did we see You as a stranger and take You in, or naked and clothe You? Or when did we see You sick, or in prison, and come to You?

"And the King will answer and say to them, 'Assuredly, I say to you, inasmuch as you did it to one of the least of these My brethren [the unborn child], you did it to Me.'"
Matthew 25:38-40

Recently, on Facebook, one of my friends posted a link to an article, "What My Escape from Hitler's Germany Taught Me About Trump's America."

The title was provocative and drew me in. However, as I read it, I realized the liberal media had so influenced the writer the article wasn't accurate. I couldn't leave a comment without a paid subscription. But her words impassioned me to write an op-ed Counterview.

I'll start with the Brett Kavanaugh hearings for US Supreme Court Justice that took place September 4-7, 2018. I closed captioned portions of the hearing on C-Span and witnessed the havoc caused by the protestors. What the media presented on TV appeared to be staged, although I had no way of knowing at the time.

However, later, I saw a video showing liberal-leaning leftists paying protestors to agitate. Someone had videotaped the exchange of money.

Before World War II, the media controlled Hitler's propaganda, just like the media controls the information that goes out over the US airwaves. They receive their marching orders from six corporations that control ninety percent of the news outlets in the US. The networks slant the news so the information (or disinformation) adheres to the Deep State's version of events. Trying to make comparisons of Trump to Hitler is ridiculous.

Hitler was a far right-wing fascist (communist by a different name). I often wondered how Hitler could become so influential in Germany when previously he was a nobody. The demonic leader had not accomplished anything worthy of news except serving jail time before running for public office.

However, historians have documented occultists predicted Hitler's meteoric rise to power and that he would become Chancellor of Germany. Dark people, like astrologers and necromancers, surrounded him, and he had a morbid preoccupation with the supernatural.

Trump is anything but that. Research it yourself.

People have accused Trump of being a nationalist, but that does not make him a Hitler. On the contrary, I hope anyone born in America or who immigrates here would take pride in our country and be thankful for what America has given them. Our language, culture, history, and Judeo-Christian heritage bind us and validate who we are: Americans. Indeed, you wouldn't call Gandhi a Hitler, for example, even though he was a nationalist.

The Bible says the Antichrist will be a world leader who comes to power by intrigue (supernaturally, like Hitler). A world order must be in place to allow his ascension.

The United Nations was the first successful attempt to unify countries with the common goal of world peace.

Another example of the ideology of the globalists is to push for open borders, leading to the refugee crisis in Europe and the swell of illegal immigration into America. Open borders take away nationalism because of the blurring of boundaries. That is the goal of the globalists: to merge the 195-plus countries into ten worldwide ruling oligarchs. Eventually, the Antichrist will ascend the pecking order, be ceded totalitarian rule, and demand all people, small and great, worship him (like Hitler did in Germany).

However, three issues specific to the United States will make it difficult for the globalists to implement their one-world government: The US Constitution, the ownership of guns, and the US Bill of Rights. If the elitists succeed in taking away our right to own guns, it will make it easier for those who have guns to control those who don't. Again, the Bill of Rights, the US Constitution, and our right to bear arms are the three most significant impediments to implementing the New World Order.

However, I think it's probably more spiritual than physical. The church's presence (Kingdom of God) through the Holy Spirit is holding back the Kingdom of Darkness. Until God removes the church through the Rapture, Satan's power is constrained, but we know the time of the Gentiles is drawing to a close.

But returning to the comparison between Hitler and Trump, Hitler's solution was to gas people who didn't fit his white Aryan race prototype. Trump is pro-life; that means all life, including the baby in the womb.

Trump is not anti-Semitic. He was behind Israel more than any other US president. That means he supports the Jews. I thank God that Trump accomplished things other presidents promised to do and didn't. We didn't vote a saint into office. We voted for someone who wouldn't kowtow to people like Kim Jong-Il, Putin, and Iran.

More recently, I hold the same view of Biden and the escapades surrounding his son, Hunter. In my opinion, all some want to do is provide juicy headlines for the tabloids and talking points for news stories that people don't listen to anyway.

I don't care what anyone in the public eye does in his private life as long as it's not illegal and doesn't impinge on our nation's security. Stories about laptops with compromising photos divert us from the critical issues plaguing our country. Maybe those "hot" topics should be relegated to the tabloids for those with nothing better to do than read gossip.

The media has become a "used car salesman with no ethics" and insulted American intelligence. Unfortunately, I have to caption all that mudslinging. Oh, how the media has changed since I started captioning twenty years ago. Of course, constant drama entices lagging viewership to stay tuned to the next bombshell. I only care that America's President is fit to serve this great nation.

The Bible also says in Romans 1:26(a):

> *"For this reason God gave them up to vile passions."*

And in Romans 1:28:

> *"And even as they did not like to retain God in* their *knowledge, God gave them over to a debased mind, to do those things which are not fitting;"*

Without God, our sensibilities as a nation have reached an all-time low. We might as well call America a modern-day Sodom and Gomorrah.

On the Palestinian issue, these people aren't refugees. That would be like saying people who moved here from Vietnam because of the Vietnam War are refugees. The Vietnamese have settled in and become part of the American fabric. And that was back in the 1970s when they came, not the 1940s.

Since Israel's founding in May 1948, the country has fought eight "recognized" wars with its neighbors. As of this writing (October 2023), Israel has defeated all its Arab (Islamic) enemies in battle.[1] In addition, the last time I read my Bible, God said He gave that land to the Jews.

If you want to make comparisons to Nazi Germany, the one worth making is the media. Think George Orwell's *1984*. If we aren't careful, soon they will have us believing doublespeak: "War is peace. Freedom is slavery. Ignorance is strength."

You will notice many articles, videos, and websites have been scrubbed from the web because they do not comport with the left-leaning media's view of the facts. However, even when people draw incorrect parallelisms, it's good to remember our past. We must not forget what happened, or the young people will believe it never happened.

I captioned President Biden's remarks on C-span addressing the Human Rights Campaign's annual dinner at the Washington Convention Center on September 15, 2018. He brought up the Kavanaugh hearing, and it was evident to me that it comes down to Roe v. Wade and protecting the life of the unborn child.

In the bigger picture, America will be held accountable for past actions regarding Roe v. Wade. I praise the Lord the US Supreme Court had the moral backbone to strike down a national law that allowed for the deaths of 64 million children since January 22, 1973.[2]

America will be judged for abortion when Jesus judges the nations. Globally, under God's New World Order, America, and all other countries will be judged in two ways, among many, but these two in particular: How they treated the innocent (the baby in the womb) and Israel.

Again, not only will nations be judged, but we will be judged individually. The media will be long gone when we stand before God and give an account of our choices, good and bad.

What will God say when you stand before Him and attempt to justify you think it's all right for a woman to kill her unborn child? Or pontificate you believe marriage between two members of the same sex is acceptable? Or there is nothing wrong with sexual relations between an adult and a minor (pedophilia).

Read the Old Testament and see what it says about the nations who sacrificed their babies to false gods. America will not escape judgment. Not only will we be held accountable for our abominable practices here, but we showed the way for the countless deaths of children in other countries that followed our example.

More recently, because of open borders and the poisoning of the mind with wickedness, we see the exploitation of children for personal gratification in child trafficking. Who could have imagined that drag queens would entertain children in schools or satanic clubs would be permitted?

Will our country be obliterated if we have a nuclear exchange? How many will die for the sixty-four million children we've murdered? I don't know, but I do know God is just. All we can do after the fact is ask for God's forgiveness.

Gone are the days of Christian prayer in public places, honoring the Ten Commandments in schools and courtrooms, celebrating Christmas with Jesus at the center, and not being afraid to exercise our free speech.

In January 2021, I captioned on C-Span the prayer spoken by US Rep Emanuel Cleaver, marking the opening of the 117th Congress. After he said, "Amen," he added, "And a woman." I thought I had misheard him and didn't write it. I was terrified to write something like that that perhaps I heard wrong, and if I didn't mishear it, I was too terrified to blaspheme my Lord and Savior. I do my job for the glory of God and will not write such adulterated words from the mouth of a blasphemer.

James 5:16b states:

"The effective, fervent prayer of a righteous man avails much."

I believe the many prayers of God-fearing Christians helped Kavanaugh to overcome all the obstacles thrown his way, leading to his appointment to the US Supreme Court.

One more quick comment: Just as God hardened Potiphar's heart when Potiphar refused to let the Israelites leave Egypt, your choices today may be your last opportunity to make those choices. In other words, once you choose, God might harden your heart to the point where you no longer have a choice. Another way of saying it is Satan will have his way because that's what you chose when the choice was yours. There comes a time when that ability to choose is no longer possible.

We live in dangerous times. Pray for the peace of Jerusalem, America, and the world.

If you haven't accepted Jesus as your Savior, do it while you still have time. Invest every minute in living out your faith at work, home, and with others. Live like you have no tomorrow.

PRAYER: Abba Father, help us to see the big picture. Sometimes, I want justice now, but there is an order to this madness that we see unfolding each day as Your return draws near.

Please help us to see the Kingdom of God at work within our hearts and on the world stage. Please use us, Lord, with all our flaws, so we can hear the words we long to hear in Your coming Kingdom: "Well done, my good and faithful servant."

Chapter Forty-One

WORLD RESET IN PREPARATION FOR THE ANTICHRIST

"The coming of the lawless one *is according to the working of Satan, with all power, signs, and lying wonders, and with all unrighteous deception among those who perish, because they did not receive the love of the truth, that they might be saved.*
"And for this reason God will send them strong delusion, that they should believe the lie, that they all may be condemned who did not believe the truth but had pleasure in unright-eousness."
II Thessalonians 2:9-12

———

Excerpt from *Seventh Dimension – The Howling: A Young Adult Fantasy*
Book 6
Seventh Dimension Series

I [Daniel] didn't say anything but glanced at the ceiling that bore a likeness to the Sistine Chapel. Colorful, hand-painted scenes from the creation story rivaled it in intensity, except this display was disturbing.

The garden scene showed Adan reaching out to touch the hand of the serpent—if you could call it a hand.

The prince's voice was smooth like silk. "It's a spectacular painting, isn't it? I brought in the finest artists from Italy. I think scenes from history, when correctly interpreted, add a lot, don't you?"

I remained equivocal. Who was Prince Adonikam? I wished I could be sure, but as he stood in front of me, I could read his mind. If he were supernatural, I wouldn't be able to. I always thought the Antichrist would not be human—perhaps a Nephilim, perhaps Satan himself, but it was hard to comprehend the Antichrist would be fully human.

A golden tree covered the front of his white thobe, matching the gold in his outer robe, and a wide, red-belted sash accented his waistline. I also noticed the gold bracelet on his right wrist. His hair was rather long underneath the keffiyeh. He was clean-shaven with olive-toned skin. His most disturbing feature was his eyes—deep, penetrating, and reptilian. Everything about him seemed...perfect, a specimen of enviable looks, intelligence, and persona.

He moved sleekly across the floor to his throne, made himself comfortable, and took a sip from his glass. After setting down his drink, his eyes drifted. A beautiful sunset hypnotized him. His words broke the silence. "I didn't have to accept this position, but the enlightened one asked me to be the leader of the New World Order."

He lifted his drink and gulped the rest of it down. Crossing his legs, he asked me again, "Do you know who I am?"

Was he testing me? I shook my head. "No."

His eyes focused on the red waters. "I have brought peace to most of the world—Europe, the Middle East, Asia, and many smaller countries. A few have sunk into chaos. They aren't worth remembering. However, we're on the precipice of our biggest accomplishment. The time has come to invade Israel." His eyes bore into mine. "As a Jew, what do you have to say about that?"

"God will prevail."

His eyes narrowed. "The ships of Chittim won't succeed this time. The United States and its allies are weaker, and my strength is growing."

"What about the United States?"

"Since the purge, their place on the world stage has—how should I say it—diminished. After Hillary Clinton won the election..." he shrugged. "The US still hasn't recovered from the EMP attack."

My ears perked up. "Trump won the election, not Hillary."

He replied flippantly. "I changed history. Do your research. Everyone knows Hillary Clinton won, not Trump, just like the United States lost the War of Independence from England."

"You can't rewrite history."

The lines of his mouth twisted unnaturally. "He who controls the past determines the future. We must control all truth and then rewrite history to where the Earth-dwellers believe my version of what happened."

I sat numb, not sure how to respond. Then I replied, "So the United States was never a free country?"

Prince Adonikam laughed. "England gave the United States their freedom. They didn't win it. That was simple. No big deal, the Mandela effect on steroids. I control the truth, the World-Wide Web, and update it to where people believe what they're told."

"Why are you telling me this?"

His reptilian eyes narrowed even more. "Because you have something I want."[1]

———

Recently, a good friend asked me to edit five pamphlets he wrote on Black Lives Matter and race relations. I spent a couple of hours going through and marking them up—basically "rewriting" them because I disagreed with his premise. If you start with a false assumption, you come to incorrect conclusions.

In my former church, I sent a YouTube video to my pastors. I said, "I hope you will watch *Critical Race Theory and Its Attack on Christianity*, presented by Pastor Brandon Holthaus with Rock Harbor Church in Bakersfield, California."

After watching it, one of my church pastors emailed me that while he had no patience for Critical Race Theory, he felt like Pastor

Holthaus allowed no room for nuance in his presentation. Therefore, if he followed Holthaus' line of reasoning, the pastor would label him a "useless idiot."

But for the grace of God go I.

The assault on our country from demonic forces is happening on every front: Our history, our culture, our freedoms, our political system, our educational system, our churches, our young people, and our future. The most disturbing aspect of all of this is many leaders and people seem unaware.

Critical Race Theory states Western civilization is a racist culture where white people have become powerful at the expense of people of color. The 1619 Project was introduced into schools to indoctrinate our young people into this "invented philosophy" from the 1980s. The postmodern philosophy has Marxism underpinnings to divide people into white oppressors and non-white victims.

Several months ago, I approached my former pastor about "victim-hood" when he stood before the church and proclaimed he was sorry for his white privilege and history of racial injustice. He encouraged us to join him in prayer over our inherited privilege and whatever social injustices we had committed concerning people of color.

I felt uncomfortable as I sat in the church pew listening to his prayer. I believed it needlessly drew attention to a supposed systemic division between white people and African Americans. I don't think—and I know some will disagree—that systemic racism exists in America.

Galatians 3:28 says:

> *"There is neither Jew nor Greek, there is neither slave nor free, there is neither male nor female; for you are all one in Christ Jesus."*

I think it's unhealthy and dangerous to force people to view every-thing through the lens of skin tone—particularly the church. The idea that Western civilization became powerful at the expense of blacks, and therefore, we live in a racist culture, is invalid.

Historically, the true Bible-believing church has done more to help enslaved people than any other group. William Wilberforce from England, for example, spent a significant portion of his life trying to end the slave trade.

I had no concept of Critical Race Theory when I spoke to my pastor about his confession of racism to the church and the corporate prayer that followed. I had never even heard of it, but deep in my heart, the whole exercise bothered me. It seemed contrived. While I agree there is individual racism in this country, to equate that to a systemic issue is very condemning and, in my opinion, demonic.

How do you convince white people in America they are racist?

First, you reach the youth through indoctrination. You rewrite Western civilization's history books to reflect a systemic record of whites oppressing non-whites.

Labeled the 1619 Project, schools have introduced textbooks that teach the first slaves arrived in America in 1619. Therefore, our country began on the backs of African slaves, without which America would not have risen to its dominance as a world power.

Second, you infiltrate the churches with a dogma that we must apologize for our white supremacy over African Americans dating back to our nation's beginnings.

More to this ideology exists, but I want to focus on these two components of Critical Race Theory, a 1980s made-up philosophy from liberal universities.

As I wrote in my book *Seventh Dimension – The Howling*, "He who controls the past determines the future. We must control all truth and then rewrite history to where the Earth-dwellers believe my version of what happened."

If scholars rewrite American history and portray Critical Race Theory as the reason for America's success, our nation's Judeo-Christian heritage will be reversed in one generation. Racism will be the dominant theme, dividing our country into whites and blacks. To think that a false narrative would serve as the basis for diminishing the greatness of what God has done for America through the toil, sweat, and bravery of our men and women for the last 250 years is an abomination to any thinking, reflective American.

I lamented my concerns in a recent exchange with a friend. Why is it before President Obama's eight years in office, there were very few issues with social injustice? I grew up in Atlanta during the Civil Rights Movement, and racial relations were a centerpiece of righting injustices spearheaded by gifted leaders who used the Bible as their framework.

However, if one goes to the BLM website, one will see that the Black Lives Matter agenda has nothing to do with what Martin Luther King preached or advocated.

Black Lives Matter and Critical Race Theory are part of a Marxist movement to cause division in our country. We know the riots and protests are being paid for and funded by the globalists (George Soros) and linked to Antifa (a terrorist organization). They aim to seize America, destroy our identity as a sovereign nation, and coerce us into a global mindset. If the globalists have their way, they will ruin our Judeo-Christian foundation, ripping the Bible to shreds.

Why is this of such concern to me? This distorted version of history and focus on the racial divide has gone beyond the educational system to an elevated role in society, sports, and entertainment. It's even seeped into the churches.

My former church bought into the social justice movement when it began, and unfortunately, it wasn't the only one. The pervasiveness of churches across America looking at this as the Gospel is startling.

When put into the context of an election season where so much is at stake (2020 and the upcoming 2024 election cycle), I found this comment at the end of a sermon unsettling:

"Please go vote, but just understand the Kingdom doesn't move forward in the ballot box. The Kingdom moves forward when the followers of Jesus follow His example and pick up the basin and the towel..." referencing when Jesus washed his disciples' feet in the Upper Room the night of His betrayal by Judas.

How could the Kingdom of God not move forward in the ballot box? The ballot box will determine the future course of our country—what happens as far as Supreme Court Justices, our policies concerning Israel, our presence or absence in the Middle East, our freedom to worship regardless of our religious affiliation, the abortion monstrosity (the deaths of 64 million babies), capitalism versus socialism, globalism versus nationalism, gender dysphoria, and issues of morality that are at the core of our Judeo-Christian heritage. Misled state, county and local institutions have already thrown Bibles out of schools and courthouses. These issues and many more are determined by how people vote and who they elect to lead our country.

The liberal-leaning Democrats shut down churches in states they controlled during the COVID-19 lockdowns, like California and Hawaii. They have continued to suppress our right to free speech. To denigrate voting and say how we vote does not move the Kingdom forward is troubling. As Christians, we have a voice in a democratic process foundational to our country's greatness.

The Democrats made race relations a central issue in the 2020 election. Even today, in 2023, the liberal-leaning Democrats want to destroy our country's framework to give them more power. Perhaps some mindless Democrats don't even know what's happening.

If African Americans believe what the Democrats tell them—that they are victims of systemic social injustice—they will never believe in themselves or God's provision to help them become great individuals. Nowhere in the world does anyone have as much opportunity as in America to overcome hardship and adversity.

It's called the Protestant Work Ethic, rooted in the Bible. Nowhere else in the world do people of all ethnicities have as much freedom to pursue their dreams as they do in America. That's why everybody wants to come here—to seek freedom, liberty, and justice.

As I said, I broached the subject of victimhood with my former pastors concerning race issues because they "bought into" systemic racial injustice. I even used my two daughters, who are from Third World countries, as an example. I raised them in a single-family household without a father. I made it clear to my daughters when they were still young that while they had much to overcome, including not having an Earthly father, God had a great future and plan for them.

However, they had to get beyond seeing themselves as victims and trust God to succeed. Only through God's grace would they be able to become the person "in Christ" God created them to be.

In the same way, if Democrats can keep the African Americans falsely believing they are powerless victims, the Democrats can control them, and that's what the liberal Democrats want—power.

However, it's even more than that. Driven by a Marxist agenda, the far-left liberals are a small but influential group who want to destroy our Constitution and remove our freedoms. They are so good at what they do their convincing arguments are hoodwinking even some conservatives. Revelation 3:20 says:

> "Behold, I stand at the door and knock. If anyone hears my voice and opens the door, I will come in to him and dine with him, and he with Me."

That means someone or something has padlocked the church—Earthly powers or people's hearts. This verse shows a spectacular, almost incomprehensible removal of true Christianity from the church in the future.

Socialism is a concerning possibility in the upcoming 2024 election. The sad thing is socialism does not allow for upward mobility. Most people don't realize it creates more greed and envy than capitalism.

Capitalism, however, tempered with Christianity, is the best form of government until Jesus reigns from Jerusalem. If the far-left wing of the Democratic party has its way, we may not even have Christian churches to attend. They may be padlocked, as highlighted in the Revelation passage above.

I believe the globalists will invent a way to bring back COVID-19 hysteria with facemasks, quarantining, and all the rest. They might launch a red flag event. Or something supernatural might happen that they would seize as an excuse to shutter churches permanently.

Perhaps a meltdown in the global economy might lead to a digital one-world currency controlled by a one-world government. I've always felt like the 501(c)(3) tax exemptions for churches could become a mechanism to close them. How many churches could survive losing their 501 charitable exemption?

I want to make a personal observation. We all have favorite pastors we admire. One of mine used to be Max Lucado. At one time, I had more books on my bookshelf by this author than anyone else.

Years ago, I began giving away most of my hard-back print books in favor of buying and storing my books on Kindle, but I kept his print books on my bookshelf because I loved his writings. That is, until recently, when I read some blog posts by him and was disappointed.

I want to end here by focusing on the upcoming election (I originally wrote this in 2020, but it applies even more now to the forthcoming 2024 election).

While President Trump may not meet Max Lucado's definition of good husband material, i.e., endued with the social etiquette you would want in your daughter's future husband, I'm glad we don't have a Mr. Rogers in the Whitehouse. (This was written while Trump was still in office).

While Lucado and other Christian leaders quickly pointed out Trump's failures and shortcomings as Christian apologists, I prefer to look at Trump's accomplishments during his four years in office. What other leader could have accomplished all that he did for America, for the unborn child, for religious freedom, for Black colleges, for Israel, and for stopping the erosion of our core Biblical beliefs in public schools, in the workforce, on college campuses, and elsewhere?

I could list dozens of examples. If you want to read them, please visit Amazon or your local bookstore and purchase *Trump's Pro-Christian Accomplishments* by Pastor Steve Cioccolanti. While every claim he made was footnoted, unfortunately, many of them have been purged/censored from the web.

Why would God bless America if we disregard the Bible and God's Word and support candidates who are anti-family, pro-abortion, and corrupt? The Kingdom of God can move forward in the ballot box with pro-Christian leaders, and in doing so, God will bless America.

Even though the Supreme Court reversed Roe v. Wade, how Christians vote in the 2024 election will be critical for our nation's survival. Will we continue to be a democracy, or will we allow the Marxists to have their way and become a socialist country?

The truth is, we need two things: We need to repent as a nation—not for our racism but for our hardened hearts, which is different for each person. While we have systemic sin, we don't all commit the same sins.

The first COVID-19 pandemic was a setup to see how far the government could go to suppress our rights as Americans and our "soul freedom" in Jesus Christ. We've seen what has happened to America under the Biden administration. Do we want four more years of what we've just endured?

Like Trump or hate him, Trump is not a globalist. He stands in the way of those who hate God, who are power-hungry, socialist-driven gluttons, and who want to "use" the uninformed and unaware to fulfill their ultimate goal of a one-world government.

That future government, predicted in the Bible, will be led by a man who comes out of nowhere—referred to as the lawless one in the Bible—and he will ultimately become the Antichrist.

If Trump were to become the next president in 2024, with his proven track record based on biblical principles (if that hasn't changed in the last three-plus years), we would have more time on God's prophetic timetable to reach souls for Jesus Christ.

In my *Seventh Dimension Series*, I embed God's redemptive love from the Cross to the midpoint of the coming Tribulation. In *Trump's Pro-Christian Accomplishments*, Pastor Steve Cioccolanti highlights Trump's prophetic role as God's latter-day King Cyrus, who helped the Jews to return to Israel and rebuild their temple. Please check them out at your local bookstore or Amazon.

Secondly, I urge Christians to vote Republican in 2024 because the Republican platform supports America's Judeo-Christian heritage. Why would a Christian vote for a platform (Democratic) that promotes the killing of the unborn child?

There is power in that innocent blood, and those of that ilk are advancing a Marxist agenda that seeks to destroy our nation (Constitution), its foundation (statues and buildings), and free assembly (Christian worship). Unfortunately, I believe many Democrats would make a pact with the devil if they thought it would keep Trump from getting re-elected in 2024.

We are on the threshold of a great world reset. God needs Christians to stand in the gap. We need to call wickedness what it is—evil and declare war on the demonic forces attacking our nation. We need Christians to wake up, and I believe the most spirit-filled Americans to lead us are the African Americans and their Bible-thumping, praise and worship churches—if they don't buy into the "lies of the devil."

Don't be deceived. Anyone who wants to divide our great nation through violence and racial tension promotes an anti-American agenda. Through our Democratic process, God has given voters the power to elect a pro-Christian, pro-American president—if there is one on the ticket.

PRAYER: Heavenly Father, I pray for Your hand on America. I pray for Your protection from our enemies, both foreign and domestic. I pray Christians will seek Your face in the 2024 Presidential, state, and local elections. May we remember the words imprinted on our coins, "In God We Trust." May our churches be filled with Your glory. May the Kingdom of God be present in our hearts. Please help us, Lord, to be faithful and true to Your Word. Let us not grow weary in doing Good Works for Your Kingdom.

Chapter Forty-Two

WHEN THEY CRY, PEACE AND SAFETY

*"For when they say, 'Peace and safety!' then sudden destruction
comes upon them, as labor pains upon a pregnant woman.
And they shall not escape."*
I Thessalonians 5:3

In the fall of 2016, I was returning from receiving a book award for *Seventh Dimension – The City: A Young Adult Fantasy* in Las Vegas. As the plane took off and I peered out the window, a small jet came out of nowhere, aimed directly at us. As the approaching plane sped closer, I saw the two men in the cockpit. *That plane is going to hit us!*

At the last second, the plane veered off and disappeared from view. I glanced around, expecting to hear other people's reactions to the near mid-air collision, but no one seemed to have noticed but me. As I tried to comprehend what I'd just seen, the flight attendant offered snacks in the aisle. When she reached my seat, I asked her, "Did you see that? A plane almost hit us."

She laughed, "Oh, that happens all the time," and kept moving.

Stunned by her reaction, I stared at her. What do you say to that? I spent the rest of the trip wondering who owned the plane.

When I returned, I did an Internet search for all American planes, commercial, private, and military, but I couldn't find a plane that looked like the one I'd seen. So I just let it go, unable to figure it out.

A few months later, I went to the RT News website to prep for an upcoming show, and to my dismay, there was the same type of plane I had witnessed in Las Vegas in a sidebar jpeg. What I saw was a Russian plane. That was impossible. Did the US allow Russian planes into our airspace?

I didn't have time to pursue that rabbit trail then, but after investigating further, I went to Shutterstock.com to buy a jpeg of a Russian plane if one was available. I was surprised to find several jpegs, and I purchased two.

As I said, this was back in 2016. How can I be sure of the date and year? Because it was one of a handful of book awards I received in person, and it was before I went through breast cancer treatment that began in January 2017 and lasted the entire year. The awards event was in October, right before the November 2016 election.

I received my somewhat dire double mastectomy surgery results when Trump was sworn into office. Ironically, I missed the swearing-in ceremony because of my doctor's appointment but captioned it on RT News that evening with Russian news commentary.

At that time, it made no sense I would see a Russian plane in American airspace, and it made less sense when Trump won the election. During Trump's term, he and Putin had a "respectful relationship."

Trump was too strong a leader for Russia to pull any shenanigans, and while captioning Russian's version of the news, I grew to enjoy the station, recognizing there was more "freedom of speech" on the Russian station than there was on American stations. Often I would caption verbatim the same news from one local news station to the next. East Coast news airs three hours before West Coast news.

Fast forward to 2022. On February 24, 2022, Vladimir Putin began offensive military operations in Ukraine on several fronts. A year later, the war continues with no definitive end in sight.

What Putin most likely perceived to be a short-term affair has turned into something far more ominous and, in my opinion, dangerous. I fear it will likely lead to a nuclear confrontation and World War

III. Because Kyiv used to be Russia's capital (formerly known as Kievan Rus), we might be witnessing the prelude to the Ezekiel 38-39 War if, indeed, the country that invades Israel from the North is Russia.

In 2016, I couldn't have imagined what the world would be like in 2023. It wasn't long after the Ukrainian War began that I had an epiphany—I suddenly realized what I saw in 2016 in the Las Vegas skies wasn't a real plane. God had given me a vision of the future.

Initially, I wanted to dismiss it. How could that be? I've always believed China was a more significant threat to the US. But maybe China and Russia were in cahoots with each other.

Once I understood the plane I saw was Russian, I became a prepper and began to buy survivor food in bulk, things I might need in a disaster, like batteries, flashlights, fire starters, extra fuel for my propane gas grill, tools to fix things, portable solar panels, and yes, I bought a gun. I also took a class to obtain a concealed weapons permit. Whatever I thought I might need in a disaster, I purchased.

I also bought a small Baofeng radio and received my technician's license as an amateur ham radio operator. Being able to communicate is crucial to me. When I learned my tech license wasn't suitable for long-distance communication (HF frequencies), I earned my general and extra license (the highest rating for amateur ham radio). Then I learned CW. I can now "talk" via Morse Code to anyone anywhere in the world. I even contacted a CW operator in Italy and recently one in England.

The bottom line is we live in highly uncertain times. Even though I am a pre-Tribulation rapture believer, God has given us an example of how to mitigate disaster in the Old Testament story of Joseph. Not everyone will prepare or heed warnings; perhaps God does not warn everyone as He warned me. I also felt like I needed to consider others and be able to help my friends and family in an emergency, which brings me to another insight I had when I was in Jerusalem a few months ago.

I was in Israel from February 27 to March 9 of this year (2023). My last trip to Israel was in January 1991 at the start of the Gulf War. The distinction between the two trips was astounding.

In 1991, Israel was preparing for war and few tourists were there. I was in Israel as a student taking a class at the Institute of Holy Land Studies, unlike my trip this year when I was touring with a church group.

In fact, in 1991, the US government asked all non-essential personnel to return to the United States. In the meantime, while I was trying to decide what to do, the school showed us how to use gas masks. That's when I decided it was time to leave.

While I realize we aren't looking at an imminent war like in January 1991, I don't believe the populace is looking for any war now or in the future. They are living in a bubble of "peace and security."

I enjoyed seeing families out at night in Jerusalem and even in the Old City. Jewish music and Middle Eastern food wafted through the breezeways. Business boomed as visitors like me went to tourist sites looking for souvenirs. There is no place like Israel, with its rich history, historical significance, and ties to Christianity, Judaism, and Islam.

It is a land of contrasts—physical beauty and spiritual significance, but a cultural enigma. How people live together in such a place is hard to fathom; yet, they live together despite their differences.

Underneath the surface, however, is a powder keg. Perhaps the Israelis have lived with such tension for so long they ignore the threat of war, trusting the government to protect their borders.

But as a Christian familiar with the Scriptures, according to Ezekiel 38 and 39, Israel will be attacked from the North. Russia is the most prominent country north of Israel. Could this war be imminent? Is Putin "Gog," as referred to in Ezekiel? In my opinion, it's more than probable. Putin is just too smart to let a good opportunity go to waste.

I pray for the peace of Jerusalem and the salvation of the Jews. It's a bitter pill to swallow as you see families living in pseudo-peace, knowing that two-thirds of Israel's inhabitants will die during the Tribulation.

> *"And it shall come to pass in all the land,"*
> *Says the LORD,*
> *"That two-thirds in it shall be cut off and die,*
> *But one-third shall be left in it:"*

I will bring the one-*third through the fire"*
(Zechariah 13:8).

I thank God I could make the trip and see those parts of Israel I did not visit in January 1991. The world is more dangerous now than it was then. Whatever God's timetable is, I pray I will be busy doing the Lord's work until the rapture. Why God gave me that vision of a Russian plane over Las Vegas in 2016 is unclear, but I'm sure it was a word of knowledge, and He meant for me to share it in the context of my recent trip to Israel.

*"But you be watchful in all things, endure afflictions, do the
work of an evangelist, fulfill* your *ministry"*
(II Timothy 4:5).

PRAYER: Abba Father, my recent trip to Israel was Your gift to me. I pray that my gift to You will be my faithfulness until You come for Your bride before the "Great and Terrible Day of the Lord." Please come quickly, Lord.

Chapter Forty-Three

THE DAY DEMOCRACY DIED UNLESS GOD INTERVENES

*"For we wrestle not against flesh and blood, but against princi-
palities, against powers, against the rulers of the darkness of
this age, against spiritual* hosts *of wickedness in the heavenly* places."
Ephesians 6:12

I considered attending the rally on January 6, 2021, in Washington DC for one reason: Trump asked his supporters to come. As I thought and prayed about it, I sensed God leading me to go.

I am a broadcast captioner, and I've spent the last twenty years providing broadcast captioning for television. Twenty years before that, I worked as a court reporter. I have reported/captioned, no doubt, billions of words from news, sports, criminal/civil trials, and depositions, which gives me a unique perspective to report what I've witnessed.

Let me add another reason for my motivation to attend the rally: In the last sixteen years, beginning with the Obama era, I have seen a degradation in news reporting—from unbiased reporting to biased reporting to complete lies.

I am glad I went to the Trump rally in Washington DC because I know the media is lying to the American people about the events of that historic day. And if they are lying about that, how can I trust them on news I personally know nothing about?

My friend and I arrived at the Whitehouse/Capitol grounds on January 6, 2021, at 7:30 a.m. When Trump's speech ended, we walked from there to the Capitol and stayed until about 5:30 p.m. The City mayor had issued a curfew, so everyone needed to vacate the area by 6:00 p.m.

Restaurants and government buildings were closed. Even the eating establishment in the hotel we stayed at, the Hyatt Regency, within walking distance of the Capitol, was closed except for takeout food.

When I returned to the hotel from the Capitol and flipped on the news, I was horrified to see what the news outlets were reporting in real-time: *Trump supporters stormed the Capitol, and people died.*

I later learned the woman shot was a veteran, and she was shot by the police, not a Trump supporter. But the media didn't say that. Why did they present the information to convince anyone watching that the Trump rally caused an insurrection and Trump had incited his followers to commit violence?

Nothing could be farther from the truth. However, nobody believed my version of events when I talked about it. Pictures speak a thousand words, so I made a video. I included every photo and video I shot in the eleven-minute video clip for one purpose: To present an unbiased, uncensored account of my experience. My friend captured the last bit of the video because my phone was out of juice when the violence started.

The video I took shows the large crowd of people, the atmosphere, and what I witnessed from 7:30 a.m. until 5:30 p.m. I listed no credits, so anyone could copy it without copyright issues. I wanted everyone to know what happened from my vantage point as an eyewitness.

If January 6, 2021, was a coup, it wasn't a coup at the behest of Trump or Trump supporters. If the truth isn't exposed by eyewitness accounts, we'll no longer have a democracy.

I believe most of the politicians in Washington DC on both sides of the aisle are corrupt. What happened on January 6, 2021, wasn't a political statement. It was a supernatural event—the battle between good and evil.

Being at the Capitol that day was deeply personal to me. My ancestors came to this country on a ship a few years after the Mayflower. I am a descendant of Anne Dudley Bradstreet, one of North America's most prominent early English poets and the first writer in the England North American colonies to be published.[1] I am a Daughter of the American Revolution and descend from many patriots who served in the armed forces.

Most importantly, I am a Christian. I will pray and support my country as long as I can. If you and I don't pray, self-serving deep-state operatives will overrun our country, and America may never recover.

The 2020 election is more than just about who won an election. It is about who we are as Americans. I'm fighting for the freedom to worship God, create stories the government won't censor, protect my family, and enjoy the privileges granted to me and you in the Constitution.

Unless we examine the 2020 election results, we aren't free. I genuinely believe usurpers stole the 2020 election, not just the presidential election but many others on state ballots, as well as those seeking lower offices in Washington DC. Maybe I'm wrong. Still, too many people believe that possibility exists.

All-out censorship began during the run-up to the 2020 election. Many questioned the election results. No one was allowed to discuss it. If you tried, they shut you up. Thousands of my Twitter followers disappeared from my account shortly after January 6, 2021. I was not allowed to speak about what I witnessed on Facebook for a couple of weeks, and even after that, few people saw my posts. I received harassing messages on Facebook. Some questioned my salvation. Members of my family wouldn't speak to me.

I called the local news station to see if I could tell my story to a reporter. No one called me back. Later, the FBI came to visit me. I was thrilled to talk to someone so I could give my first-hand account.

One important question they asked me was, did I go inside the

Capitol? I did NOT go inside the Capitol on January 6, but there were people—and I don't know who they were—encouraging the crowd to enter, claiming, "It's the people's building. You're entitled to go inside."

I said, "No, I will stay here. I'm as close as I want to get." I was close enough to videotape and observe what was happening, and after seeing one patriot pepper sprayed for getting too close or entering, I didn't want to go any closer. The young man, in his late teens or early twenties, was in great pain, and I did not want to risk it.

I have to ask, though, what would have happened to me if I had gone inside? It's scary to think about it because other Trump supporters innocently entered, and they paid dearly.

If you look at the last three years objectively—if that is even possible—it's obvious we have two standards in this country: One for the Democrats and one for the Republicans. Demonization is rampant on both sides and upsetting for any American who loves this country.

As I've said before, the battle that day was supernatural, and America was the loser. How many spies mingled among the crowd? How many thugs stirred up trouble? I saw Antifa members or Black Lives Matter folks dressed in black. Your guess is as good as mine as to who they were, but they were the bad actors. I witnessed it.

"But Jesus knew their thoughts, and said to them; 'Every kingdom divided against itself is brought to desolation, and every city or house divided against itself will not stand'" (Matthew 12:25).

To think there could have been any coordinated effort by Trump followers to cause an insurrection is ludicrous. There was no Internet access the entire day. The servers were down, or people were blocked from posting.

An insurrection would need to have been instigated by people who knew a lot more than those around the Capitol building, and I can tell you it wasn't anyone like me; i.e., gray-haired women, babies in strollers, old men who could barely walk, or Chinese folks handing out pamphlets warning about the CCP. I knew nothing bad had happened until I returned to the hotel around 5 p.m. and turned on the local news.

I also have a question three years later no one has adequately answered. Where were the police? More security is present at the DisneyWorld entrance than was present that day at the Capitol.

If you listen closely, near the end of my video, you can hear patriots crying out in response to the violent acts against the Capitol. You can see a patriot take down one of the violent men.[2]

Three years later, the whole story of what happened on January 6, 2021, has never been told. I've lost confidence the public will ever know. The media and the pundits in control of the narrative have suppressed the truth.

When I asked God what book He wanted me to write after I finished *The Night Cometh: 20 Fantastical Short Stories,* He said, "I want you to write about January 6, 2021."

I immediately said, "No, God. I don't want to write about that, not after what I went through when I returned home." Besides, it wouldn't last one day on Amazon because of censorship.

I was at a coffee house when I had this internal conversation. I was all set to do some writing. Instead, I packed up my computer, went home, and napped. I was not going to write about January 6, 2021.

That was in the early part of 2023. Here I am, in September 2023, writing the book God told me to write, but it's hidden inside a broader book about *God's Good Works.* Jesus said in Matthew 10:16:

> *"Behold, I send you out as sheep in the midst of wolves. There-*
> *fore, be wise as serpents and harmless as doves."*

I believe God always provides a way to accomplish His purposes.

PRAYER: May God bless America. May God protect Christian believers despite growing persecution. May God keep our families strong despite constant attacks on traditional family values.

I pray for revival, for God to heal our land from COVID-19, wickedness in high places, and corrupt powers that cast shadows on our future. May we find favor in the Goodness of the Lord. Let us not lose heart. The Kingdom of Heaven is coming soon with all the power, glory, and majesty of our Risen Savior. Please help us, Lord, to be ready!

Chapter Forty-Four

THE GREATEST DUPE IN AMERICAN HISTORY – PART 1

"The wisdom of the prudent is *to understand his way, But the folly of fools* is *deceit."*
Proverbs 14:8

As I wrote in the previous chapter, there is no doubt in my mind Trump won the 2020 election on November 3. I saw sufficient evidence of documented cases of voter fraud from multiple unbiased sources. I saw videos by experts demonstrating how the votes were flipped on the Dominion voting machines from Trump to Biden. And if I hadn't downloaded those videos off YouTube, I wouldn't have access to them now. YouTube deleted most of them for "violating YouTube guidelines."

I'm not stupid; you aren't either if you put on your thinking cap. Why would YouTube remove all those videos?

Consider this: Why did every media outlet in America (excluding some small conservative/independent stations) refuse to talk about possible voting irregularities? Not only did they refuse to talk about it, they repeatedly said there was no voter fraud.

Media as far away as France reported, "There is no voter fraud." And this was before the accusations were made. I captioned an

English-speaking French news station the day after the election, and they said repeatedly, "There is no voter fraud." If you repeat something enough times, people believe it.

Why would Biden supporters and the media not listen to experts who had evidence that vote flipping occurred—even though connecting the machines to the Internet was illegal? Evidence revealed the vote flipping resulted from foreign interference.

Why did Facebook and Twitter delete posts that questioned voting irregularities?

Why did the Supreme Court refuse to take the cases presented by Texas, Sidney Powell, and others, and dismiss the claims based on standing, which is simply a procedural way to avoid looking at the incriminating evidence?

Why would Facebook, Twitter, Instagram, and other social media websites de-platform Trump? Why would they remove thousands of Twitter followers from my account and the accounts of many American patriots?

The most important question is, what were Biden supporters afraid of? If Biden had won, wouldn't they want transparency? Wouldn't they want proof so the "fallacious" claims of Trump supporters could be debunked?

Pundits claimed dozens of courts had the evidence, and there was no election fraud. The courts had the evidence but never looked at what was submitted. Is that justice? Is that righteousness?

The Court of Heaven knows the truth, and that's why I struggle. Why did God allow a usurper to be President after so many prayers were offered by American patriots? Why did God choose not to reveal the truth to the American people?

I was maligned mercilessly for being there on January 6, accused of participating in the insurrection—even by friends.

I watched and listened to all the speeches on a makeshift videoboard near the Whitehouse before making the 30-minute walk to the Capitol Building.

Almost three years later, I'm skeptical of many news stories and rarely caption news. Perhaps in hindsight, news anchors and reporters during the 2020 election cycle and COVID-19 pandemic were in the

same predicament as me: Forced to speak and write the official narrative without regard to whether it was true.

However, for reasons I don't understand, God did not reveal the
truth. Perhaps God is allowing the far left-leaning socialist Democrats
to take down this country. We know the United States must diminish
as a world power. This great nation of the last two hundred years is not
mentioned anywhere in the Bible in the final days before the Lord's
return. To put it plainly, we're absent from the scene of world events as
if we never existed. This saddens me because I love my country.

Perhaps some of those who attacked me were simply deceived.
People can also have so much disdain for the truth they reach a point
of wickedness where God gives them over to reprobate minds (Romans
1:28).

Examples like Potiphar (God hardened his heart, Exodus 9:12) and
Saul (the Spirit left him, I Samuel 16:14) are enough to put the fear of
God in me.

I have seen more hardness of heart recently than in my entire life.

Here's an example. A woman who needed a wheelchair was in the
Jacuzzi at the gym. I had helped the same older woman the previous
week to get out of the Jacuzzi into her wheelchair. Her aide couldn't do
it alone. I was doing laps in the pool when I noticed the woman trying
to exit the water.

I stopped swimming and shouted above the noise, "Do you need
help?"

The woman said, "Yes. Could you, please."

I climbed out of the pool and went over to lend a hand. Two young
men were just a few feet away in the same Jacuzzi. They turned their
backs, pretending not to notice this large, disabled woman who needed
help getting back into her wheelchair. Moments like that make me
realize the depravity of human hearts.

I had the same feeling when I was at the Capitol, as men dressed in
black holding long iron rods attempted to destroy the Capitol
windows. Not just one man but many.

I yelled, "No," and others shouted "Antifa."

Why would anyone want to damage the Capitol of the greatest
country in the world? Jesus said in Matthew 24:12:

*"And because lawlessness will abound, the love of many will
grow cold."*

When it comes to nations, perhaps the vilest form of government
is communism. One only needs to objectively examine the Democratic
Party to see its decline from American liberalism a few years ago to the
depravity that consumes it today.

Sanctioning the murder of the unborn child, tearing apart the traditional family, legalizing same-sex marriage, pushing climate change as a
form of religion, weakening our country by limiting the use of our
natural resources, encouraging illegal immigrants to enter our country
through the Southern border, demonization of white people for
supposed systemic racial prejudice, sexual perversion, transgenderism,
and they have even taken a page from the Chinese Communist Party's
script to implement social credit scores to limit our freedoms. My
heart cries, "What's wrong with these people?"

God chose not to intervene in the 2020 election, so we have a
usurper in the Whitehouse. I hope those who interfered in the election process are held accountable. There is nothing worse than a guilty
conscience (if they are still human). Power is fleeting, and evil haunts.
As individuals and as the Body of Christ, we must recognize what's
happening.

Unfortunately, those who refused to look at possible election
tampering in the 2020 election have greatly diminished the trust of the
American people in our democratic system. Some individuals in key
positions could have paused the certification and didn't, i.e., Vice President Pence.

Many states violated their own state constitutions and election laws
(Pennsylvania and Georgia), and the US Supreme Court was unwilling
to hear the cases presented to them. Not a single Democrat would
look at the evidence. They said, "Nothing here, move on."

As of September 2023, much of the voting fraud evidence from the
2020 election has been scrubbed (censored) from the Internet, and
now the 2024 election looms. Perhaps since everything turned out so
well in the 2020 election, the Democrats will follow the same game
plan: Create another virus, order lockdowns, allow unlimited voting by

mail-in ballots, close schools, demand face masks, and scare people into receiving more vaccines.

The FDA has already issued an emergency use authorization for vaccines for the next pandemic. How convenient is that for the 2024 election?

The media is as responsible as those in power. Complicit reporters are part of the future beast system that will capture the world when the anti-Christ reigns and demands worship. Who puts a mic in front of speakers so the masses can hear them?

> *"And he was given a mouth speaking great things and blasphemies, and he was given authority to continue for forty-two months"*
> *(Revelation 13:5).*

Over the next couple of years, I anticipate the persecution of Christians and Jews and an inching toward communism (unless the Lord intervenes). The power-hungry, left-leaning Democratic leaders will tax us to death and confiscate our property. Inflation will become rampant. World War III looms as Ukraine is losing the war with Russia.

Do I expect the results of the 2020 election to be overturned? Putting my hope in people who say it could happen is unrealistic. I've seen nothing to make me optimistic even one individual might be willing to look at the evidence.

That day has long passed, and people have moved on. But I do have hope in my Lord and Savior justice might happen before the complete demise of this great nation. I want my country to be deemed worthy of Jesus' one-thousand-year Millennial reign from Jerusalem.

In the meantime, I keep looking up, praying hard, and hoping God will bring as many people into His Kingdom as possible. The church flourishes during persecution, and that's what's important now.

Nothing remains hidden forever. Could a Civil War erupt when people realize the media and leaders duped them? Could we face a national catastrophe that might kill many people? I don't know how far the US will fall, but it's nonexistent in the Book of Revelation. Maybe the rapture takes out half the population. I hope so. I hate for anyone to perish, but half is probably wishful thinking.

Keep looking up and pray for God (through His Bible-believing church) to reach as many people as possible. Each day that passes is one day closer to the Lord's return. As the Bible says, the end of all things is near (I Peter 4:7). That ending will be glorious for those on God's side.

PRAYER: Dear Jesus, our hope is in You, not political candidates. Until You return, I pray Your wisdom from above will guide us into all truth. We praise You, Lord, in "whom there is no variation or shadow of turning" (James 1:17b).

Chapter Forty-Five

THE GREATEST DUPE IN AMERICAN HISTORY - PART 2

"...above all, taking the shield of faith with which you will be
able to quench all the fiery darts of the wicked one.
"And take the helmet of salvation, and the sword of the Spirit,
which is the word of God; praying always with all prayer
and supplication in the Spirit, being watchful to this end
with all perseverance and supplication for all the saints—"
Ephesians 6:16-18

When did things take a downward spiral toward violence on January 6, 2021—sometime between 2:30 and 4:00 in the afternoon. Men dressed in black holding long iron sticks emerged from the crowd on the side of the building I was facing. They climbed the Capitol steps and took their position in front of the Capitol windows.

When a patriot took down one of the thuds, another thud would replace him, and another patriot would haul that one to the ground. If it weren't for the patriots, the damage to the Capitol would have been extensive. One of those brave patriots was a woman. I wish I knew who she was. I would tell her, "Thank you."

I saw police officers earlier in the day around the Capitol, but there was no law enforcement anywhere when the violence started.

I saw one young man, about 18 or 19, who had been pepper-sprayed. If the Capitol police were pepper-spraying trespassers, why didn't they stop the attack on the Capitol?

An EMS tech set up a stand next to me to help anyone who needed medical help. What organization was she with? I don't know. People brought the young man to her for treatment. By that point, my phone was out of juice, and she offered to charge my phone.

The crowd was not wild, as the media proclaimed. At least from what I could see from my vantage point until the violence started. I am not sure if I was on the South or the West side of the Capitol but my video would make that clear to anyone who is familiar with the area.

A few smoke bombs went off sending up smoke near the Capitol to my right. Some people were crawling up the sides of the Capitol steps. That was the only hint of anything amiss, but not enough to cause me to be concerned for my safety.

Singing, praying, laughter, patriotic voices, and the outward demonstration of love for our country is what I witnessed. I saw Christians witnessing and handing out tracts. Chinese attendees were sharing pamphlets warning about the CCP.

Older adults, young people, children in strollers, men and women filled the expanse. Crowd estimates range between one and two million. I saw a couple of men dressed strangely, but the people, for the most part, appeared to be freedom-loving Americans who felt as I did —that the Democratic Party stole the election.

I hoped by my presence to encourage those in charge of the certification to consider an audit of the election returns. Perhaps when the House of Representatives saw such a huge crowd, they might be willing to look at the evidence.

I never saw any violence except for the guys dressed in black in front of the Capitol. (When I say front, I'm not sure if that was the East side or the South side). I captured it on my phone until my phone went dead.

However, the media has misled the public into believing every person at the Capitol that day committed acts of violence. And to impeach Trump on trumped-up charges of insurrection is insanity. To the contrary, Trump supporters saved our Capitol.

Because the Internet wasn't working, nobody knew what had happened inside the Capitol, at least no one to whom I talked. It was very late by the time I heard the proceedings had stopped hours earlier.

The biggest issue for me is what the media has perpetuated—that the "rioting" and breach of the Capitol was Trump's fault. Trump said nothing to incite violence on January 6, 2021, in his speech from the Whitehouse to his supporters.

As the Apostle Paul said in II Timothy 4:7:

> *"I have fought the good fight, I have finished the race, I have kept the faith."*

I'm sure no Bible-believing Christian today would accuse Paul of inciting violence. However, if you know your Bible, there were instances when the crowd became a mob upon his arrival. And that's because the Jews hated Paul. They wanted to discredit, destroy, and send him away. Can I say it? They wanted to kill the Apostle Paul because they hated his message.

In the same way the people who hated Paul made up stories about him, the people who hate Trump have conjured up that same hatred, accusing him of things they themselves have done. It's called projection. And, dare I say, demonic influencers have caused the Democrats (and some Republicans) to commit unpatriotic acts that, in my opinion, are vindictive.

What other words can one use to describe the ridiculous impeachments? There is too much wickedness in all of this to call it by any other name. And since they failed to convict Trump in the second impeachment trial, they are on a witch hunt now to destroy him. The Democrats are trying to pass a bill to prevent Trump from being buried in Arlington National Cemetery. What would motivate American citizens to be so hate-filled?

Someday, if America survives, historians will look back with disbelief at what these vile, wicked leftists have done. There is always hope with God, but each day, I see more and more stupidity. I can't believe this is America. It's not the one I knew. It's turning into China.

I won't vote again unless nonpartisan experts examine the Dominion voting machines. Too much evidence has been revealed to lead any thinking, unbiased individual to believe votes were switched from Trump to Biden. Many computers, documented as changing votes, had IP addresses in other countries like Italy and China.

Anybody looking at Mike Lindell's docs-movie entitled *Absolute Proof* has to ask: Is Biden a legitimate president?

Evil has a way of pricking souls and turning people into miserable creatures. Left to their own devices, Democrats and elitists involved in these shenanigans will destroy themselves. They will never have peace. Proverbs 5:22 says:

> *"His own iniquities entrap the wicked* man, *And he is caught in the cords of his sin."*

The biggest question is why God would allow what happened to play out as it did? If you look at the evidence—which has not been examined by the Supreme Court, the media, the Washington pundits, the political left, and those who hate Trump—you might be surprised by what it reveals.

Why would God allow a usurper in the Whitehouse? Why would He allow the elitists, the media, the Democrats, and the cabal to suppress the evidence of Trump's almost undeniable win?

Look at all the executive orders Biden issued in his first month in office. They were anti-Christian, globalist-driven, and pregnant with Marxist ideology.

While some want to rewrite our rich history and treat our Constitution with contempt, pack the Supreme Court, and allow every illegal soul to enter our country regardless of what crimes they have committed, most Americans didn't vote for this.

As one looks at the Middle East—the instability already taking root because of Biden's weak leadership/appeasement, a realignment of power in the Middle East points to the Ezekiel 38-39 War. Again, why would God allow all of this to happen?

God finally told me, "For the same reason, I will allow the anti-Christ to come on the scene and pretend to be the world's savior."

As I contemplated what God spoke to me, I would also add I believe a reckoning is coming, a separation of the true believers from the fake ones. We also know the Ezekiel 38-39 prophecy must be fulfilled.

Since Biden took office, I've seen the demolition of America one executive order at a time. I see a pack of wolves devouring our freedoms and silencing the voices of those who love our Lord and Savior. I have even seen deceived "Christians" who have bought into the fake religion of political correctness, Black Lives Matter, Critical Race Theory, tribal prejudice, and socialism. Nominal Christians might as well be sheeple because of their inability or unwillingness to "test" what they hear and see if it aligns with Scripture.

I urge Christians and those who are questioning what is happening —i.e., the censorship of conservative thought, the destruction of our national heritage by tearing down statues, rewriting American history and skewing it with an underlying agenda to create ethnic unrest, violating our Constitution (i.e., not following the election laws in several states), the indoctrination of our children in schools with godless ideologies, denigrating the family unit, confusion of gender, killing the unborn child even up to nine months, the worship of the planet instead of the worship of God, and the unwillingness or the cognitive inability to call evil, evil, and good, good—to speak out, to be bold, to be a witness for Christ, and to be fearless in the face of darkness.

If the Lord tarries, persecution is coming. And that persecution will be even sooner if we sit back and let what is happening to America continue. We are watching the erosion of what makes America great.

Are you kneeling for Black Lives Matter? Get up off your knees. Are you voting to support the right to kill a baby in the womb? Switch parties. Are you doing your own research to validate whether what the media is telling you is true? Be a Watchman on the wall. Are you reading your Bible every day? Be a Berean. Are you praying for your country, for wisdom in high places, and for God's truth to reach those who don't know that truth?

> *"The effective, fervent prayer of a righteous man avails much"*
> *(James 5:16b).*

Jesus Christ is the answer—not tribal autonomy, not celebrating Black History Month, not drawing distinctions between African Americans, Caucasians, Chinese, or any other ethnic identity.

> *"There is neither Jew nor Greek, there is neither slave nor free, there is neither male nor female; for you are all one in Christ Jesus" (Galatians 3:28).*

We wouldn't have racial division or inequality if everyone took this verse to heart. The answer to racial issues is Jesus Christ. America would be far better off if churches focused on that instead of apologizing for their whiteness. If churches took to heart Biblical principles that are not man-focused but God-focused with a Biblical worldview, we could heal our streets and land.

I leave you with this thought. We know God ultimately wins, but in the looming battle, I see many casualties. Globalism doesn't care about individual rights, freedoms, or accountability. The elitists care about power. The communists care about control. The socialists care about themselves. Anyone in their path that they can manipulate, they will. They call the uninformed useless idiots. An idiot is somebody who doesn't know what's happening. If you are reading this, wake up.

Don't be deceived. Don't believe the lies of the far-left. The CCP (Chinese Communist Party) is out to take control of this country, and if I were a betting woman, I bet they will do it without firing a shot. They want our resources, and anybody who gets in the way of their political agenda is just collateral damage. They care nothing about you or me.

The man sitting in the Whitehouse is a Chinese puppet, bought and paid for with Chinese money. And when he's no longer useful, they will get rid of him and put in Kamala Harris or some other brainless puppet.

Imagine the hoopla when the first black woman is in charge. Never mind that she's a communist; she's black and a woman with a Marxist ideology. Don't believe me? Do your own research.

My hope is in my Lord and Savior, Jesus Christ. The one good thing is that Biden's agenda will hasten our Lord's return. As you read this, I urge you to make sure you are a born-again Christian. If you have any doubt, pray this prayer:

———

"Heavenly Father, I know I am a sinner. Please forgive my sins. I believe your Son, Jesus Christ, died on the cross for me. I ask You to come into my heart, and help me to live my life for You. In Jesus' name. Amen."

———

If you prayed that prayer and believe it with all your heart, you are now a Christian. Today is the first day of the rest of your life, both here and into eternity. Get a Bible and start reading. Join a church. And make it a priority to spend time in prayer with Jesus each day. Guard your heart against the evilness that is all around us. The Lord's return is soon. Stay steadfast. Keep looking up, and fight the Good fight.

PRAYER: Dear Jesus, help us not to grow weary while doing Good, for in due season, You will reward us if we do not lose heart (Galatians 6:9.)

Chapter Forty-Six

TRUTH AND DECEPTION IN THE LAST DAYS

"But the word of the LORD endures forever. *Now this is
the word which by the gospel was preached to you.*"
I Peter 1:25

I could not have imagined on January 6, 2021, what the world would be like two and a half years later. That we would suppress the results of the election seemed unfathomable.

What about the censorship of other facts—not only connected with the election but also with the vaccine? How can we know the truth about anything if we can't have open discourse?

I couldn't have imagined the indoctrination of Critical Race Theory, the focus on sexual dysphoria, and the insistence on vaccinating children for a virus that rarely injured them. I couldn't have imagined the level of censorship our country has endured. I couldn't have envisioned our freedoms being trampled upon.

Who gave Washington permission to vilify me and others because we didn't want an ineffective and dangerous vaccine? Many people aren't aware of the COVID-19 vaccine-related injuries. Who could have imagined the high-handedness of governmental actions

restricting the use of life-saving drugs like Ivermectin and Hydroxy-
chloroquine in favor of Remdesivir?

Do the doctors not have some degree of culpability for not
speaking out? Many of those deaths labeled "COVID-19" were due to
kidney failure from being treated with Remdesivir.

Deception has been rampant in every facet of our lives. Another
example is the continued false climate change narrative bordering on
religious fanaticism.

One of my favorite Bible passages is when Pontius Pilate asked
Jesus:

"What is truth" (John 18:38a)?

Whether Pilate's question was in jest or genuine is prophetic
because Jesus said deception would mark the last days. Pilate's only
comment after questioning Jesus is when he spoke to the raucous
crowd (incited by the Jewish leaders):

"I find no fault in him [Jesus] at all" (John 18:38b).

When Jesus' disciples asked Him in private about the end of days,
"Tell us, when will these things be? And what *will be* the sign of Your
coming, and of the end of the age?" (Matthew 24:3), Jesus replied:

"Take heed that no one deceives you" (Matthew 24:4).

I believe Jesus spoke of the time in which we now live. We see the
very things Jesus described to His disciples. Many things must occur
before Jesus' return. Yet, of all the things He could have said, His first
warning was, "Take heed that no one deceives you."

If the Christian church today (referred to in Revelation as the
Laodicean Church) is as deceived as it seems, what can we expect when
the many signs that Jesus listed happen in the next few years?

For example, what about when Christians in the West face persecution? We've never had more than "soft" Christian or Jewish persecution in the United States.

As I watched Trump supporters on January 6, 2021, physically take down men dressed in black, (probably Antifa), I saw those brave men and women as heroes. But what followed was not an affirmation of their acts of bravery.

Instead, an attack was launched on the very people who stood up to evil and risked their lives to save the US Capitol.

Some people entered the Capitol building peacefully, and a few caused disturbances. Still, they were unarmed, and, in my opinion, those who were disorderly might have been planted there by operatives on the inside.

The distortion of what happened on January 6 is an example of what Christians can expect in the future. I anticipate Christians will be targeted, accused, tracked, and imprisoned by government officials. For what? Whatever fits the narrative at that time. Truth is now relative in the eyes of those in power. We will become targeted like the Jews were in Germany.

How do I know this? Because Jesus said this would happen. He told His disciples in Matthew 10:22:

> *"And you will be hated by all for My name's sake. But he who endures to the end will be saved."*

In the Bible, the first instance of a Jew disobeying the government is when Moses' mother hid her baby in the reeds of the Nile River. Even back then, rulers were "hell-bent" on killing babies, the most vulnerable members of any society. Ecclesiastes 1:9 says:

> *"That which has been is what will be, That which is done is what will be done, And there is nothing new under the sun."*

Did Jesus advocate socialism in His teachings? Absolutely not. If you read the parables, you will see Jesus often referred to work.

After God created Adam, one of God's first commands after putting Adam in the garden was for Adam to work it and keep it:

*"Then the LORD God took the man and put him in the garden
of Eden to tend and keep it" (Genesis 2:15).*

Jesus also modeled a work ethic that would put most of us to
shame. When He was only twelve, He told his parents when they
found Him in the temple.

*"Why did you seek Me? Did you not know that I must be about
My Father's business" (Luke 2:49)?*

*"For even when we were with you, we commanded you this: If
anyone will not work, neither shall he eat" (II Thessalonians 3:10).*

Jesus said to his disciples in John 9:4:

*"I must work the works of Him who sent Me while it is day;
the night is coming when no one can work."*

I don't doubt that another deeper night of darkness is coming
when work will be impossible. Specifically, in the words of Jesus, Christians will not be able to witness, speak about God, quote Scripture, or
worship.

More broadly, Proverbs 16:27 states:

*"An ungodly man digs up evil, And it is on his lips like a
burning fire."*

If you force people to be unproductive and feed them a carrot with
government handouts, you create an environment rife with discontent,
complacency, and laziness.

Socialism goes a long way toward giving people a sense of entitle-
ment. We are commanded to embrace hard work, and through our dili-
gence, we can tithe for the Kingdom and even have some left over to
share with those in need.

"What is truth?" Pontius Pilate asked Jesus. Is there not a voice inside your head telling you the Truth? Or is your conscience so seared you can no longer hear the Truth? Or is your comfort more important than believing the Truth?

> *"For the wrath of God is revealed from Heaven against all*
> *ungodliness and unrighteousness of men, who suppress the*
> *truth in unrighteousness, because what may be known of*
> *God is manifest in them, for God has shown* it *to them"*
> *(Romans 1:18-19).*

Where does Ketanji Brown Jackson, the first black woman to serve on the US Supreme Court, stand on gender issues? Was she able to define a woman?

What Ms. Jackson said is on record in Washington DC, but what you say about this topic is recorded in Heaven's Book of Remembrance.

When Jesus returns, He will open those books. Every act and thought has been written to the minutest detail, and God's books are far more accurate than I could record as a court reporter, even with my top credentials.

I would urge anyone who has not read the Book of Revelation to read it. Revelation is the only book in the Bible that promises a blessing:

> *"Blessed* is *he who reads and those who hear the words of this*
> *prophecy, and keep those things which are written in it; for*
> *the time* is *near" (Revelation 1:3).*

The Bible is more relevant than people think.
Acts 17:28 :

> *"for in Him [Jesus Christ] we live and move and have our*
> *being, as also some of your own poets have said, 'For we are*
> *also His offspring.'"*

And Colossians 1:17:

"And He [Jesus Christ] is before all things, and in Him [Jesus Christ] all things consist."

If you haven't thought about the end times, now is the time. Each of us should be a Berean and search the Scriptures. That is the only way to know what is true and what is false. God has given us a template to live by, and His Truth is as pertinent today as when it was written thousands of years ago.

If the Bible isn't relevant, why did countries seek to ban it throughout history? Do you know why the Dark Ages are called the Dark Ages? From 500 AD to 1500 AD, governments forbade people to own a Bible, and the Apostate Church burned Bibles.

History repeats itself. The New World Order will implement a reset, and the Globalists will seek to destroy true Christianity. In the name of a fake religion (climate change), they will martyr Christians to reduce the population. Spurned by Satan, they will seek to end the lives in which the Word of Life indwells.

Why does the New World Order want to reduce the population? I hope it is evident to those who love the Lord that God, in the beginning, provided adequate land and resources to support all the human beings for which He would give His life. It is a lie to say the Earth can't sustain the people God created.

Satan hates human beings. Depopulation in the form of abortion, plagues, war, and starvation—among others, serves the evil one's agenda.

Anyone he can deceive is a likely target. If Satan had his way, no human would survive.

Jesus stated in Matthew 24:22:

"And unless those days were shortened, no flesh would be saved;
but for the elect's sake those days will be shortened."

Another critical point is this: The Word of Life (Holy Spirit) cannot indwell a person who is not fully human. Suppose the devil's goal is to corrupt the human genetic genome. As stated above, in Ecclesiastes 1:9:

> *"That which has been* is *what will be, That which* is *done is what will be done, And* there is *nothing new under the sun."*

At the time of Noah, the fallen angels corrupted the bloodline of humanity:

> *"Now it came to pass, when men began to multiply on the face of the earth, and daughters were born to them, that the sons of God saw the daughters of men, that they* were *beautiful; and they took wives for themselves of all whom they chose"* *(Genesis 6:1-2).*

> *"Then a third angel followed them, saying with a loud voice, 'If anyone worships the beast and his image, and receives* his *mark on his forehead or on his hand, he himself shall also drink of the wine of the wrath of God, which is poured out full strength into the cup of His indignation. He shall be tormented with fire and brimstone in the presence of the holy angels and in the presence of the Lamb. And the smoke of their torment ascends forever and ever; and they have no rest day or night, who worship the beast and his image, and whoever receives the mark of his name'" (Revelation 14:9).*

> *"And men were scorched with great heat, and they blasphemed the name of God who has power over these plagues; and they did not repent and give Him glory" (Revelation 16:9).*

Is the Holy Spirit unable to bring some Earth-dwellers to repentance during this time? Perhaps it's not possible. Jesus died for humankind, not Chimera, Nephilim, trans-humans, robots, or any combination above.

As the elitists become more emboldened, deception will reach a tipping point. Some of those who have been "sleeping" (lazy) will wake up. They will recognize the evil lies and start to push back.

I see signs of that happening now. Truth always wins in the end because God always wins. Following these events, censorship and persecution will increase.

When the globalists realize they can no longer operate with the power they gifted themselves during COVID-19, they will have to develop other ways to take away our freedoms.

The Internet most likely will be sabotaged and rebuilt with Christian websites/links removed. The only information on the World Wide Web will be what the Globalists want people to know. The church will go underground, like in China.

An excellent book on Christian persecution is *Live Not by Lies: A Manual for Christian Dissidents* by Rod Dreher, Adam Verner, et al.

What happens then will be evident to those who swallowed the red pill (*The Matrix*), but those who took the blue pill will live in the deception matrix.

The Tribulation is coming, and it will last seven long, horrific years. Everyone in the world will be affected on a broad scale, but in a biblical sense, the Day of Jacob's Trouble is to bring the Jewish people back to Israel and God. When the Great Tribulation is over, Jesus will take His rightful place on His throne in Jerusalem.

How soon until our Lord's return? No one knows, but God has given us His Word, which provides a startling account of these last days. Almost one-third of the Bible is devoted to prophecy. God has not left us without the ability to know the future.

The number one sign of Jesus' imminent return is the reconstitution of the Jewish State in Israel. While Israel was born in a day—

> *"Who has heard such a thing?*
> *Who has seen such things?*
> *Shall the Earth be made to give birth in one day?*
> *Or shall a nation be born at once?*
> *For as soon as Zion was in labor,*
> *She gave birth to her children"*
> *(Isaiah 66:8).*

—birth pangs are increasing, heralding the return of Jesus as King. The ultimate rebirth of Israel will be when Jesus reigns from Jerusalem.

Those referred to as Earth-dwellers in the Book of Revelation, after the Rapture, will endure seven years of hell on Earth. Some will repent and accept Jesus as the Messiah. They will share the Good News for the glory of God until Jesus returns. Millions will be martyred.

The truth is, however, in the last days, most will fall away.

According to I Timothy 4:1:

> *"Now the Spirit expressly says that in latter times some will depart from the faith, giving heed to deceiving spirits and doctrines of demons..."*

Amos 8:12 states:

> *"They shall wander from sea to sea, And from the north to east; They shall run to and fro, seeking the word of the LORD, But shall not find it."*

Bibles, Christian books, writings, magazines, blog posts, articles, signs, pamphlets, and anything Christian worldwide will be almost impossible to find. Because the Word indwells us as the Holy Spirit, I wonder if that means Christians will also be rare.

In my opinion, that points to the rapture taking place before the seven-year Tribulation begins. However, that doesn't mean Christians won't endure trials. Suffering refines faith, separating the wheat from the chaff, revealing true faith from comfortable Christianity. But Christians will be spared God's wrath.

Next time you listen to a news broadcast or someone pontificating about something important, ask yourself, is that person speaking the truth?

While the world will get darker, as prophesied in the Bible, God's light can shine through you and me and be a witness to our Savior's sacrificial love. In the upcoming days, God will help us to survive and even thrive.

Satan's goal is to separate you from God. Governments come and go. Hollywood stars rise and fall. Countries conquer, and others disappear from maps. Money has wings and flies away. If you have not accepted Jesus Christ into your heart, do so now. Repent and start living for Christ as if you have no tomorrow.

PRAYER: Dear Jesus, even when we grow weary, please help us to persevere. Goodness can still be found, and it's worth the fight for Your Glory.

Chapter Forty-Seven

YOU AREN'T IN KANSAS ANYMORE

A Christian Satire on the Deplorable State of Affairs

> *"And you* He [Jesus] made alive, *who were dead in trespasses and sins, in which you once walked according to the course of this world, according to the prince of the power of the air, the spirit who now works in the sons of disobedience."*
> Ephesians 2:1-2

August 27, 2021
My Dear American Patriot,

I know you're perplexed about the deplorable state of affairs and what in the world is happening. I want to reassure you, my friend. You're not in Kansas anymore. You will never go back to Kansas. Why would you want to go back to that cesspool when Trump was president, when America was energy independent, when the economy was thriving, when no one knew what Critical Race Theory was, when drag queens didn't entertain youngins in grammar school, and before the rigged election? After all, we know Biden is our Commander in Chief. As they said, "Nothing here, move on."

Aren't you glad nobody has been able to check those Dominion voting machines? I wouldn't allow it—they are under my dominion. We needed everything in place for the New World Order. It will be even better than the famous novel Brave New World. By the way, I helped Aldous Huxley write that book. He wrote it exactly as I instructed, and look how famous he is.

Depopulation has been going quite well. The blood of the babies offered to Molech gives me substantial supernatural power to share with my hopeful benefactors. Your utmost care is critical, my little messengers. Keep supporting me at the abortion clinics. I will repay you in kind on Judgment Day. Isn't it nice to be on the winning side? We've made tremendous progress since we got rid of Number 45.

Now, to more important things: Don't let the troop withdrawal from Afghanistan concern you. The news media is lying to you about all those casualties. You know how they lie about everything. They rarely get anything correct, and this is their biggest blunder yet. Just keep your eyes on me; don't look up. I control the powers that be in Washington. You need not concern yourself with matters so high and mighty.

Don't believe things are looking up? Think about all the free money you've received since my cat's paw landed in the office of the presidency. Many of you haven't had to pay rent in months. Ah! An extended vacation. You say, "Keep this gravy train going." I say, "Let the government take care of you. You deserve it. Let's make America great again. After all, the mantra is 'land of the free.' That should include free housing, free health insurance, and free food."

But back to the current situation. Many of you have been dismayed about forced vaccinations at your job and vaccine passports, the harbinger of war in the Middle East, and the terrible plight of illegal, helpless people crossing the border into the country.

However, this is all necessary to discourage believers. We want them to join us. We must reeducate them about what's really happening. We need to convince the recalcitrant that borders are evil. In due time, they will come around. Once they realize nobody is listening, they will shut up. Christians are like sheep. Eventually, they do what they're told. That's what Christians do. That's what the Good Book tells them to do.

Rest assured, we're gaining strength and growing in numbers. The world theater is poised for me to send my world ambassador on the scene. He's a man of fortresses, and he will usher in world peace. Once we kill off a significant portion of the population through every means at our fingertips—like pestilences and climate change and same sex marriage—we will build back better with

15-minute cities. What a great way to imprison people without them knowing it.

In the meantime, we need to destroy the US Constitution. That document has caused more damage to the blacks, Latinos, and LGBTQ community than any other document in the history of humankind. The next presidential election should seal that deal.

I thank my minions who put those dominion voting machines in strategic locations. I expect to have complete dominion over all the countries that are members of the United Nations after the next US presidential election. My chosen leader is already here setting up a one-world government. My craftiness, cunning, and deceptive persuasion have allowed the pieces to fall into place.

We must keep up climate change hysteria. Population control will go a long way toward reducing carbon emissions, and we must reduce beef consumption. Cows produce too much flatulence and contribute to the worst pollution. Killing the cows will eliminate four percent of the greenhouse gases worldwide. Let's give our diminutive mindless idiots something to cheer about.

For this news cycle from my lofty position as Prince of the Power of the Air, here're my recommendations:

1 Make sure you receive the COVID-19 shot. In fact, make sure you receive all the booster shots . The more, the merrier. They are for your good. Fear is a good motivator. Keep scaring those who are resistant into compliance.

2 Follow all CDC, NIH, and WHO guidelines. You

know they have your best interest at heart. You know they wouldn't recommend a vaccine that hadn't undergone rigorous testing. They would never compromise, would they? After all, they have no liability if someone dies from COVID-19.

Sheeple can't see the connection because—well, they are sheeple. They are too absorbed in themselves, taking selfies and looking for cheap electric cars. Seriously, we don't have to tell the public about the adverse effects of the shot—just tell them they won't get COVID-19. If you say it enough times, they'll believe you. Everyone hates bad news. Just give them good news—the shot works. That's all you have to say.

3 Make sure you wear your mask. You wouldn't want to infect your loved ones, would you? After all, the death rate is as high as 1% in people who are too old to be valuable citizens. Again, do the right thing. Wear your mask. Make your children wear a mask. You want them to be good, compliant citizens like you when they grow up. You want to teach them to obey every law passed by Big Brother because that's what good citizens do.

Be a good role model; never question anything—that's bad. Always trust the government. You know the Warlords care deeply about you and your family. Trust them with all your heart and lean not on your own under-standing.

4 Keep your eye on your neighbor, colleague, spouse, and cohort like a private investigator. We need to make sure everyone does what's best for the country. If

someone doesn't follow the rules, you must report them to the authorities. We need to cancel those who distort the truth. If someone doesn't comply, we may need to take bolder measures, like implementing a social credit score. I can vouch they have been very effective in China to force people into compliance. I'll share more about that later.

Remember, Big Brother is watching you. Be ready to embrace the new reality. The IT Matrix is under construction even as we speak. You aren't in Kansas anymore.

Signed by the Prince of the Power of the Air, Lord Lucifer

PRAYER: Dear Jesus, please help us not to believe the devil's lies. While we can't go back to the way things were, we can glorify You in our hearts and in what we say. People need You, Lord, and we have the Good News they are dying to hear. Give us strength, Lord; the Kingdom of God is here.

Chapter Forty-Eight

STRANGER IN A STRANGE LAND

"But seek first the kingdom of God and His righteousness,
and all these things shall be added to you."
Mathew 6:33

While hard to admit, recently, I've found it challenging to write. The world is so upside-down; where do you even start? And when your "creative works for the Lord" become the target of removal from the web due to censorship, you wonder, "What difference can I make?"

YouTube struck down my video of my trip to Washington, DC on January 6, 2021, claiming copyright infringement. Of course, we know that was a cover-up for the real reason—censorship. My video didn't comport with what the Washington bureaucracy wanted the public to believe happened that day.

Almost three years later, the only acceptable narrative is Trump supporters caused an insurrection on Capitol Hill.

I shot the raw footage myself except for a tiny clip my friend who accompanied me gave me. I edited nothing, not even when I video-taped sideways unawares. I made no narration and used one Bible quote from Isaiah 5:20:

"Woe to those who call evil good, and good evil; Who put dark-
ness for light, and light for darkness; who put bitter for
sweet, and sweet for bitter!"

I've included the link to the video for anyone who wants to watch it. It's currently on Rumble (hidden) and later will be uploaded to my website.

CLICK ON THIS LINK: Lorilyn Roberts' video from January 6, 2021, Capitol Hill

I wrote a reply to YouTube (they never responded), explaining I created the video as a first-hand account of what I saw and witnessed that day for historical purposes. I've never made a cent from any videos I've uploaded to YouTube, and my subscribers, the last time I checked, are less than a hundred. But YouTube felt the need to take it down. Why?

There are days I struggle not to be down about the world's affairs. I used to love to caption news as I felt my skills to write the spoken word glorified God. I could help the deaf or hard of hearing know what was happening in real-time as if they could hear the words themselves. I spent decades developing and perfecting the skill. Thousands of briefs live in my head to help me write at the extraordinary speed necessary to caption live words said by reporters in as little time as possible.

Then COVID-19 hit. I'll spare you the details. But the news changed. No longer was it news—it was one narrative from every news station—almost verbatim, whether I was captioning local news out of California, Connecticut, or New Mexico.

That meant every local news outlet was receiving information from the same source. I questioned—is this a free press? What about people who disagree?

At the same time, the suppression of information questioning the election results took the nation by storm. The absolute "word" on the news beat was Biden had won, and anything to the contrary was a conspiracy theory or Trump supporters suffering from derangement syndrome.

Then, the vaccine became available, and the push was to get every living human vaccinated. They probably would have vaccinated dead people if they thought they could get money from it. I'd never seen such over-the-top, in-your-face propaganda in my long life (and I can say that now). I'd say it's unprecedented in American history. I'll say one thing about that: It was never about vaccines.

The turning point in all of this for me was personal. One evening, I was captioning a segment about vaccines, and the reporter said repeatedly the vaccine was safe for pregnant women. As I was writing his words and my captions were being read by millions of people in real-time, I knew what I was writing was a lie.

Whether the vaccine is safe for anybody is open to question. But the COVID-19 vaccines were never tested on pregnant women. So, how can you make such a statement?

I thought about the six million Jews and the two hundred million others Adolph Hitler murdered in concentration camps and gas chambers. Hitler didn't personally kill those people. He had little Hitlers who did it for him—who carried out his orders without question, forcing the Jews into the gas chambers, poisoning them, and then stealing their meager belongings. Where was their conscience?

They must have known what they were doing was wrong. How can you kill someone who has committed no crime and not have guilt convict you? Romans 1:28b says:

> "...God gave them over to a debased mind, to do those things which are not fitting;"

God pricked my conscience, "You are writing words you know aren't true. You're spreading lies using the gift of writing I've given you in a way that doesn't glorify Me."

I never understood the power of evil—until then. It is easy to say, "I was just doing my job." You fill in the blank. My job of providing closed captioning was now requiring me to write lies. Was I going to keep doing this? If so, how was I any different from a Nazi?

Once God convicted me, I couldn't do it anymore. I quit writing local news. Someday, I will stand before God and account for every word I've uttered and every word I've written. I asked God to forgive me.

However, I thought it would be okay to write conservative national news. So, I volunteered for several hours of Fox News—Sean Hannity, Tucker Carlson, Laura Ingraham. I captioned one hour of Tucker Carlson, and my modem broke. Then, programming mysteriously disappeared from my schedule. I questioned the schedulers, and no one knew where those shows went or why they removed them.

Shortly after that, I remembered something I'd forgotten. On election night, I was captioning election results for a California local station, and I had Fox News on to monitor the national front. Fox News was the first station to call several critical states for Biden when it made no sense. They led the way in announcing the shutdown of counting returns. I knew this had never happened before because this was the fourth presidential election I had captioned. I sensed something nefarious in the works.

After that strange set of events, I concluded God didn't want me to caption news. The truth is all the traditional American news outlets are different "legs" or "arms" of the same corrupt news organization(s).

There is a burden that comes with knowing the truth. Matthew 11:30 comes to mind. Jesus said:

"For My yoke is *easy and My burden is light."*

Jesus does not give us burdens we can't bear. But I feel like a stranger now in this world where truth is so elusive, and many who I thought were Christians might be tares and not wheat.

We are living in the last days. What did we think these days would look like? A walk in the park? Anyone who says we can usher in the millennium without Jesus might as well believe in the New World Order. What's the difference?

I'm pointing this out because the subtlety of error in interpretation is demonic. Looking at eschatology in the Bible only through the lens of symbolism requires one to throw out most of the Book of Isaiah (many chapters are devoted to the Millennial Kingdom with Jesus

Christ reigning from Jerusalem) and the Book of Revelation (prophetic).

What does God require of us?

> *"He has shown you, O man, what is good;*
> *And what does the LORD require of you*
> *But to act justly,*
> *To love mercy,*
> *And to walk humbly with your God"*
> *(Micah 6:8).*

We are blessed to see the beginning of the birth pangs harkening the return of Jesus. To do the things He has gifted us to do means we must occupy until His return.

What has God called you to do? Do it!

Despite social media attempting to silence me, I will keep writing. I will keep speaking the truth. Even though the world's burdens are immense, God has called me to carry His light burden. I will share the Gospel when it's easy and when it isn't.

God needs all of us to be a light, no matter how big or small. In the unity of Christ, we can shine brightly among a world of lost souls.

> *"For God so loved the world that He gave His only begotten*
> *Son, that whoever believes in Him shall not perish but have*
> *everlasting life" (John 3:16).*

Inspiration can go a long way toward reviving a weary soul, encouraging those circumcised hearts in Christ to keep on keeping on.

Be blessed.

PRAYER: Dear Jesus, please help us to make a joyful noise unto Your holy name. Help us to give thanks in all things. Please help us remember all we have You have graciously given to us. You will return any day to set up the Kingdom of Heaven in Jerusalem, Israel. Lord, I long to worship You in person as we see that day approaching. Please, come quickly, Lord Jesus.

Chapter Forty-Nine

THE BLESSED HOPE AND THE FEAST OF TRUMPETS

"...looking for the blessed hope and glorious appearing of our
great God and Savior Jesus Christ."
Titus 2:13

Do you know the return of Jesus will most likely occur in autumn? In Genesis through Leviticus, God lays out His prophetic timetable.

Unfortunately, after centuries of pagan influence, liberal Bible translations, and a lack of Old Testament understanding, most Christians are unaware of the significance of God's appointed times. God said in Hosea 4:6a:

"My people are destroyed for lack of knowledge."

In Genesis 1:14:

"Then God said, 'Let there be lights in the firmament of the
heavens to divide the day from the night; and let them be for
signs and for seasons, and for days and years;'"

In this passage, "seasons" refers to "appointed times or festivals," not the more familiar meaning of spring, summer, fall, and winter.

The Jews celebrate seven festivals or appointed times—but they are not Jewish appointed times; they are God's appointed times. Unfortunately, when Constantine changed the official calendar from a lunar calendar to a solar calendar, our "Christian" holidays merged with pagan holidays. In the process, Christianity absorbed many pagan traditions.

For example, Christians celebrate the resurrection of Jesus at Easter. Historically, this day coincides with a pagan holiday following the flood and the Tower of Babel. Easter, because it's set according to the spring equinox, is often days apart from Passover and Jesus' crucifixion.

Christmas is another Christian celebration mired in pagan practices. It originated in Egypt long after Jesus' birth and resurrection. The first recorded date of Christians celebrating Christmas did not occur until 336 AD. A few years later, Pope Julius I established December 25 as the date for Christmas and Jesus' birth. This became the second date on the Christian calendar to be associated with a pagan holiday.

Jesus said in Matthew 15:9:

> "And in vain they worship Me, Teaching as doctrines the
> commandments of men."

Through God's appointed times, we see the timeline of Jesus' ministry. Just as He fulfilled the first four festivals at the time of His first coming, so will He fulfill the remaining three feasts at His second coming. In Leviticus 23:4, God said:

> "*These* are *the feasts of the LORD, holy convocations which you*
> *shall proclaim at their appointed times.*"

While we are not obligated to keep the festivals in the church age, knowing what they mean has enriched my Christian walk. The sound of the shofar blowing reminds me of the Feast of Trumpets. All around the world, in recent years, people have heard mysterious trumpet-like noises coming from the Heavens. You can listen to these sounds on YouTube.

Could these trumpet calls be announcing the Lord's imminent return? Knowing three of the seven festivals remain unfulfilled gives me heightened awareness that Jesus could return at any moment.

If you long for His return as I do, thinking about these things brings a quickening of the spirit. As saints have cried through the centuries, "How much longer, oh, Lord, until your return?"

I have listed below the seven Levitical Feasts and their meanings in reference to the Messiah. Remember, feasts (moadim) in Hebrew mean "appointed times."

———

1. Feast of Passover – Fulfilled at Jesus' first coming. Jesus is the Passover lamb. His sacrifice occurred at the very hour the high priest slaughtered the lambs within the temple.

2. Feast of Unleavened Bread – Leaven is a picture of sin in the Bible. Jesus was in the grave for three days and three nights following His crucifixion as God's unleavened, spotless Son. He was the perfect sacrifice for our sins.

3. Feast of First Fruits – Jesus was the first to be resurrected. In I Corinthians 15:20, Paul refers to Jesus as the "first fruits of those who have fallen asleep."

4. Feast of Weeks (Pentecost) – Occurred fifty days after Passover. On Pentecost, Peter preached from Jerusalem, and 3,000 people responded to the outpouring of God's Holy Spirit, sparking the beginning of the Church Age in which we live.

5. Feast of Trumpets – While the first four feasts were fulfilled at Jesus' first coming, most Bible scholars believe the last three will be fulfilled at His second coming. The Feast of Trumpets is the first of the fall feasts. Many believe this is the feast when Jesus will rapture the church from the Earth. In I Thessalonians 4:16, Paul wrote:

"For the Lord Himself will descend from heaven with a shout,

with the voice of an archangel, and with the trumpet of
God. And the dead in Christ will rise first. Then we who
are alive and *remain shall be caught up together with them*
in the clouds to meet the Lord in the air. And thus we shall
always be with the Lord."

The first day of the Jewish New Year is the Feast of Trumpets. The Jewish New Year, also known as Rosh Hashanah, falls on the calendar dates of 1 and 2 Tishrei.

In 2023, that started on September 15 at sundown and concluded at nightfall on September 17. In 2024, the date for Rosh Hashanah begins at sundown on October 2 and ends at nightfall on October 4.

While we do not know the exact date of Jesus' return, that day is fixed at an appointed time. If you look at the signs Yeshua gave in the Olivet Discourse in Matthew 24, He tells us what signs to look for that would mark His return. He wanted us to prepare for His coming. In Matthew 25:1-13, in the Parable of the Ten Virgins, He warns us what would happen if we didn't.

6. Day of Atonement (Yom Kippur) – Many associate this day with Jesus' physical return to Earth following the Great Tribulation. On the Jewish calendar, Yom Kippur occurs on 10 Tishrei. In 2023, that began at sunset on September 24 and ended at nightfall on September 25

In 2024, Yom Kippur falls on the Gregorian calendar on October 11, beginning at sundown, and ending at nightfall on October 12. Zechariah 12:10b says:

"...then they [the Jews] will look on Me whom they pierced. Yes,
they will mourn for Him as one mourns for his only son,
and grieve for Him as one grieves for a firstborn."

7. Feast of Tabernacles or Booths – Looks ahead to when Jesus will reign from Jerusalem over all the Earth for one thousand years (Micah 4:1-7).

———

As the return of Jesus draws near, I always look at the unfulfilled fall feasts knowing this might be the year. The Feast of Trumpets would most likely be the appointed time for the rapture.

Knowledge of God's fixed days assures us that even though Gentiles have altered the calendar, forgotten God's appointed times, and imbued the Christian faith with pagan practices not found in the Bible, God never changes. His return is set—if not this year, maybe next year—in 2024, 2025, 2026 or beyond. Regardless of the year, when autumn draws near, I remember—and hope, this is the "appointed time."

PRAYER: Dear Jesus, help us to keep looking up and not lose heart as the world devolves into chaos. We know You will return at the appointed time, and we wait expectantly for the Blessed Hope.

Chapter Fifty

ARE YOU READY FOR A.I. IN A POST-CHRISTIAN WORLD?

"Now when these things begin to happen, look up and lift up your heads, because your redemption draws near."
Luke 21:28

What would happen if enemy combatants took down the Internet? Or our trusty iPhones were rendered inoperable by malware? Or China invaded Taiwan. Would the US be next? Or what about Russia? It seems like everyone wants to blame Russia for everything. Did you notice Putin's expression when he conversed with Biden face-to-face? What did the autocrat's eyes tell you? Putin is not a dummy.

Did you hear the audio recording of someone feeding Biden the answers to questions at a press conference before being removed from YouTube?

Or maybe it's not China or Russia that wants to take us out. Perhaps it's Iran. Several colorful countries worldwide would love to see America brought to its knees.

That got me thinking, what if—you can fill in the blank.

Barring God's divine intervention, America will be like all the other great nations in human history. They all had a limited lifespan of 200 years or less. Invading armies destroyed them, or the countries succumbed to internal collapse because of moral decay and depravity.

Will we survive as a nation? I hope so. God is a gracious, merciful God, but He is also a righteous King. America will only survive if we ask for God's forgiveness, repent of our sins nationally, and forge a new path based on Biblical principles. Unless we do that, God has numbered America's days. God would not be just if He didn't.

It doesn't take a rocket scientist to figure out the United States is in deep trouble, and we don't have a national leader with the fortitude to stand up to the far-leaning left in Washington, the globalists' climate change agenda, Deep State oligarchs, or religious fanatics who hate America. We had that person in Trump in 2019. Five years later, I'm unsure if Trump is still that man.

Anyone who tries to turn the nation back to what our Founding Fathers envisioned knows the powers that be will "cancel" him. There is only one thing left to do—destroy the US Constitution.

Big Brother is increasingly watching every move we make with the help of artificial intelligence. Scientists frame it in the context of convenience and innovation.

Have you noticed how Siri and Alexa help you to be lazy? These robotic voices listen to what you say. They make you dependent on them once you start using them, and they give you the information they want you to trust. It may or may not be accurate. It's censored data. So, without a repentant spirit, our nation goes caput.

That brings me to my next question. What would you do if the floodgates of wickedness were suddenly unleashed on America? Do you have food stored up? Do you have a water source you can tap into? Do you have alternative energy available? Could you live without going to the store for toilet paper and soap?

I think everyone should own a gun and know how to use it. That was my gift for my birthday when I turned 62. I never thought I would need one. I figured I'd call 911, and the police would immediately arrive at my house. That's what I used to believe until I captioned a news broadcast in Orange County, California. Rioters were breaking into stores, stealing commerce, and destroying buildings. The police stood by and did nothing.

We will soon enter the Tribulation described in the New Testament, specifically in the Olivet Discourse in Matthew 24 and 25, Mark 13, and Luke 21. War is coming to the Middle East, and our freedoms will increasingly become more restricted. The God-hating globalists, left-leaning liberals, technocrats, and anti-Christian socialites on social media are canceling Christians.

I wanted another way to stay in touch if the Internet went down or my phone was useless. Please don't believe it can't happen. I used to have landlines until they quit working. AT&T wouldn't service them. Things you never thought imaginable are happening. I tell myself I can't be more surprised by anything, but then I am when something that seemed unimaginable only a couple of years ago happens.

Don't believe COVID-19 is going away. The three-year COVID-19 pandemic was a worldwide manufactured plandemic and will happen again in 2024. Why? Because it's another election cycle in the US.

In the Bible, pharmakeia carried the idea of sorcery, occultism, and black magic. In this sense, Paul used the term in Galatians 5:20 as "witchcraft." Revelation 9:21 and 18:23 translate it as "sorceries." [i]

I want one thing: I want freedom. I don't want someone forcing me to take a jab or two jabs or ten jabs. I don't want someone listening to my phone conversations or prying into my personal life. I don't want my tweets censored or my Facebook posts removed by twits who think they know more than I do.

Don't silence me because you think I'm writing something offensive. Freedom-loving soldiers died to give citizens like you and me that right. Christians and conservatives need the right to point out the elephant in the room or to say, "The emperor has no clothes." If it weren't so serious, it would be humorous. But no one is laughing because it's not funny. It's scary.

It begs the question, what can you and I do? While it might seem insignificant, the most important thing Christians can do is pray. And pray some more. God never tires of us communing with Him. And keep looking up, knowing that the devil is working overtime because he knows his time is short (Revelation 12:12).

Satan will attack anyone vulnerable. We must protect ourselves spiritually. We must claim the name of Jesus to put a wedge between ourselves and the world. Only then can we be wise. Wisdom comes from God and God alone.

> "The law of the LORD is perfect, converting the soul; The testi-
> mony of the LORD is sure, making wise the simple"
> (Psalm 19:7).

> "Jesus said, 'Behold, I send you out as sheep in the midst of
> wolves. Therefore be wise as serpents and harmless as
> doves'"
> Matthew 10:16.

What does this have to do with my becoming a ham radio opera-tor? There is a connection. The simple fact is I don't trust the govern-ment. With my general ham radio license, I can communicate with anyone worldwide. There is no way any government or any country can control all the airwaves because virtually every country uses them on the planet.

It's one tool in my arsenal. On a broader scale, we need to consider what we need to survive if everything goes down. The glob-alists want to make middle-class America poor and dependent on government handouts. Be dependent on yourself and not the govern-ment. Almost always, unless it's in the context of Biblical grace, whenever someone gives you something, there is a catch. It's not free.

The masterminds of the New World Order control the bureaucrats in Washington. They have one agenda: Control. Why? Because they have sold their souls for greed, power, perversion—you name it. Ninety-nine percent of the political pundits care nothing about you or me. They care about their egos. They have enriched themselves at the expense of those who pay their exorbitant salaries through taxes.

Why do you think the political leaders and the world's elitists hate Trump so much? Why do you think 90 percent of the media speaks the same narrative? Whatever happened to divergent opinions that counter political insiders? I've said this repeatedly throughout this book: All the major news outlets in the United States are owned by a handful of companies pushing a globalist agenda. Globalists want power. They want a one-world government.

If you aren't convinced the media is lying about COVID-19 or what happened in Washington DC on "Insurrection Day," wise up. Ask God to open your eyes. Pray for yourself, your family, your neighborhood, your city, and country. God is on the side of Truth. On whose side are you?

Forgive my ranting. Somebody needs to rant. God will call somebody else to do it if it's not me. We need God-fearing Christians to exercise their voices on what matters to God. Gone is the time to be agreeable. There is nothing pleasant about socialism or communism. Big Brother through A.I. wants to own you.

Make sure you have on hand several months' food supply. Have a resource for bartering, like silver. Purchase the silver that's referred to as "legal tender." Don't rely on the greenback. You can't continue to print money, dole it out, and expect it to retain any value.

Other bargaining items might be bullets, freeze-dried food, water, survival gear, and, most of all, Bibles.

Get your radio technician's license and preferably your general radio license (for longer distances) so you aren't dependent on the Internet for information. Whatever information you read on the web will be increasingly censored.

And to access those 5G towers, the phone companies will tell you to upgrade your phone to use them. They will tell you how superb 5G is: You can use it to control the lights in your home, feed the dog, wash your dishes, and start your coffee—yes, what a fantastic world we live in when we need those props to survive.

I watched a ten-minute video on the virtues of 5G. If you want to be lazy, go for it. Let those A.I.s invade your home and take control of your life. Become a puppet on the strings of convenience. Know that comfort comes with a price. Big Brother (A.I.) is watching you.

I heard Pastor Billy Crone make an interesting reference to something Jesus said in the Olivet Discourse.

> *"Let him who is on the housetop not go down to take anything out of his house"*

Matthew 24:17.

What a strange thing for Jesus to say. Why not go back to your house? Is there a backdoor to that high-tech TV in your living room, iPhone, or computer? Why would someone be standing on his housetop anyway? Could it be to scan the sky to see if drones are spying on you? That's what they do in China.

A.I. is watching you. "It" knows what you're doing all the time. Once fully implemented, 5G will enable even more government control, and medical passports will be deemed "necessary" to travel. Do you want the government to know your medical history?

The folks at the top of the coming "beast system" will pass government mandates everyone must follow, starting with compliant companies. 5G-enabled health technologies will revolutionize patient treatment, but there is a downside: Do you want your private health information available in the cloud via an app on your iPhone?

Medical passports are coming. If you are non-compliant, where will it lead? Imagine a car that can smell your breath to determine if you've taken the vaccine. No vaccine, your car won't start. Even today, the unelected medical complex has proven it can force companies and people to kowtow to their demands. None of this is by coincidence.

I'm only scratching the surface. I could say more. Don't dither around wondering where to start. Just start. It would be best to entertain the mindset that you need to prepare for war. It's that simple. And remember, China wants our resources. They want Silicon Valley, Hollywood, agricultural land, and technology.

They don't want to blow us to bits. They will take us over through stealth and not with nuclear missiles. Those missiles will land in the Middle East. The Ezekiel War could happen at any time. Read Ezekiel 38 and 39 in the Old Testament. Ezekiel, a Hebrew prophet, wrote it 600 years before the birth of Christ.

Ham radio is a healthy and simple way to stay in contact with those you love and folks worldwide. It's not hard to learn, and it's been around for a long time. There are thousands of ham radio operators in the United States. And I'm sure other countries have many as well. Take an online class; I passed the three levels of licensure on the first try, and I'm not "wired" that way (pun intended). On January 6, 2021, I didn't know the first thing about ham radio.

My advice is to avail yourself of every opportunity to be self-sufficient. You don't need to be paranoid. You need to be, as Jesus said, as harmless as doves and wise as serpents. Be prepared for the unexpected; don't believe most of what you hear. Avail yourself of independent sources for information. Most importantly, keep looking up. Trust God. He's got this!

Jesus said in Luke 21:28:

> *"Now when these things begin to happen, look up and lift up your heads, because your redemption draws near."*

If you don't remember anything else I've written here, remember this: Jesus is coming soon. Don't leave Earth without Him.

PRAYER: Dear Jesus, please help us to be the person You created us to be. We need wisdom that surpasses human understanding to survive in this post-Christian world. We need You, Lord, to make it through each day for Your glory.

[i] Dr. Johnson, Scott. "Pharmakeia: Sorcery, Witchcraft, Pharmaceutical, Pharmacy, Pharmacist & the Roots of Modern Day Drug Industry." http://ernestlmartin.com/images/Pharmacy,%20Drugs,%20Sorcery,%20IG%20Farbin.pdf

ABOUT THE AUTHOR

Lorilyn Roberts is the author of fifteen books, including the award-winning *YA Seventh Dimension Series* and memoirs *Children of Dream*s and *Tails and Purrs for the Heart and Soul.* After scuba diving around the world and earning her college degree studying abroad, she settled into single motherhood, adopting two daughters from Nepal and Vietnam. She later earned a Master of Arts in Creative Writing and is president of the Gainesville, Florida, Chapter of Word Weavers International. Lorilyn has rescued many orphaned dogs and cats, and when she isn't writing books, she provides broadcast captioning for television. In her spare time, Lorilyn is a ham radio operator and CW/Morse Code enthusiast. KO4LBS.

ALSO BY LORILYN ROBERTS

The Night Cometh: 20 Fantastical Short Stories

LorilynRoberts.com

Children of Dreams

As an Audiobook

Tails and Purrs for the Heart and Soul

As an Audiobook

———

THE DONKEY AND THE KING
(A Story of Redemption)

Lorilyn Roberts
Illustrated by Linda S. DiFranco

Look for the hidden word "good" on every page.

The Donkey and the King: A Story of Redemption

"Wonderful story with positive Christian values. Loved the illustrations. It's a hit with my kids!"

—"Goodreads" reader

Young readers become world leaders.

<u>Book Love</u>

"Book Love is beautiful inside and out. Roberts uses a child to teach children the love of books and it works beautifully. This book is a must for elementary classrooms and libraries. I highly recommend Book Love by Lorilyn Roberts if you have a child wanting to learn to read."

—Joy Hannabass, Readers' Favorite Reviewer

SEVENTH DIMENSION SERIES

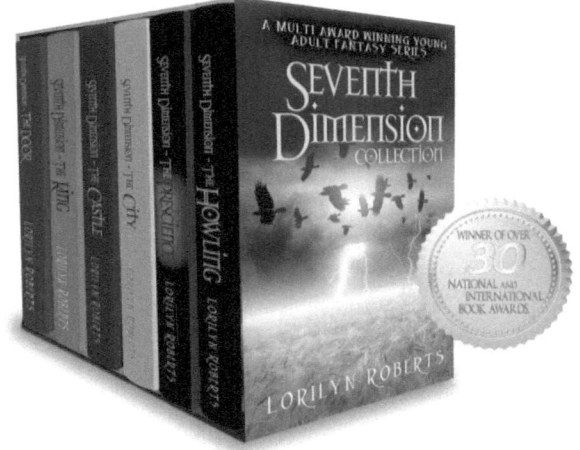

LorilynRoberts.com

Seventh Dimension - The Door, Book 1

As an Audiobook

Seventh Dimension - The King, Book 2

As an Audiobook

Seventh Dimension - The Castle, Book 3

As an Audiobook

Seventh Dimension - The City, Book 4

As an Audiobook

Seventh Dimension - The Prescience, Book 5

As an Audiobook

Seventh Dimension - The Howling, Book 6

As an Audiobook

———

ADDITIONAL BOOKS

LorilynRoberts.com

Food for Thought Cookbook

Seventh Dimension Devotional Series: Am I Okay, God?

NOTES

5. BORN AGAIN IN THE KINGDOM OF GOD

1. Lorilyn Roberts

7. WRETCHED, PITIFUL, POOR, BLIND, AND NAKED

1. Hoffman, Mary. *Amazing Grace*. Frances Lincoln Children's Books, 2007.

23. MOSES SPOKE OF THE RESURRECTION

1. Roffman, Barry S., "Resurrection, Reversing Time & DOD Monitoring Here." Updated 5-23-18 and 7-25-21. https://www.arkcode.com/photo4_18.html

37. BRAVE NEW WORLD OF COVID-19 AND THE COMING MARK OF THE BEAST

1. https://www.facebook.com/jeremy.ramsey.737/videos/10223958741418609/?t=159
2. Valuetainment COVID-19 "Heated Vaccine Debate - Kennedy Jr. vs Deroshowitz, Moderated by Patrick Bet-David. YouTube https://www.youtube.com/watch?v=IfnJi7yLKgE&t=251s

38. HITLER AND COVID-19 - THE PARALLELS ARE STARTLING

1. The Mel K Show Mel K. and Dr. Bryan Ardis on the Global Medical Killing Fields & Crimes Against Humanity. BitChute. 2-15-22. https://www.bitchute.com/video/CmUHSylD29W7/

40. TRUMP, BIDEN, MEDIA, GLOBALIZATION, ISRAEL, ABORTION, AND HITLER

1. List of wars involving Israel. (2023, June 20). In *Wikipedia*. https://en.wikipedia.org/wiki/List_of_wars_involving_Israel
2. Tobias, Carol. "More than 64 Million Unborn Children Have Died Since Roe v. Wade." National Right to Life Protecting Life in America Since 1968. January 20, 2023. https://www.nrlc.org/communications/more-than-64-million-unborn-children-have-died-since-roe-v-wade/

41. WORLD RESET IN PREPARATION FOR THE ANTICHRIST

1. Roberts, Lorilyn. *Seventh Dimension – The Howling: A Young Adult Fantasy, Book 6.* (Gainesville, FL: Rear Guard Publishing, 2019), 89-90.

43. THE DAY DEMOCRACY DIED UNLESS GOD INTERVENES

1. Homage to Mistress Bradstreet, John Berryman, Faber and Faber, 1959. Wikipedia. Last updated August 31, 2023. https://en.wikipedia.org/wiki/Anne_Bradstreet
2. Roberts, Lorilyn. The Day Democracy Died Unless God Intervenes. Rumble. January 2021. https://rumble.com/vcsjrt-the-day-democracy-died-unless-god-intervenes.html